Teaching Writing Skills

with

Children's Literature

Connie Campbell Dierking
Susan Anderson-McElveen

MAUPIN
HOUSE

Teaching
Writing Skills

with

Children's Literature

Teaching Writing Skills with Children's Literature
Connie Campbell Dierking
Susan Anderson-McElveen

Design and layout: *Billie J. Hermansen*
Cover: *David Dishman*

Dierking, Connie Campbell, 1956-
     Teaching writing skills with children's literature ' Connie
Campbell Dierking, Susan anderson-McElveen.
       p.   cm.
     Includes bibliographical references.
     ISBN 0-929895-27-4
     1. Language arts (Elementary)--Study and teaching--Activity
programs. 2. Children's literature--Study and teaching
(Elementary)--Activity programs. 3. English language--Composition
and exercises--Study and teaching (Elementary) I. Anderson
-McElveen, Susan, 1956- II. Title.
LB1576.D4643 1998
372.62'4--dc21   98-36568
                                               CIP

Also by Connie Campbell Dierking and Susan Anderson-McElveen:

Literature Models to Teach Expository Writing

Maupin House Publishing, Inc.
PO Box 90148
Gainesville, FL 32607-0148
1-800-524-0634
fax: 352-373-5546
info@maupinhouse.com
www.maupinhouse.com

Maupin House publishes classroom-proven language arts resources for innovative teachers K-12. Call or write for
a free catalogue.

Printed in the United States of America

10 9 8 7 6 5 4 3 2

Dedication

To Mom and Dad, my personal cheerleaders,
Maddie and Andrea, always an inspiration,
and to Mark, my ever-patient husband.

C.C.D.

To my parents for introducing me to the gift of books,
my husband, Scott, for his support,
and my students whose enthusiasm in sharing their words
have taught me so much.

S. A. M.

Acknowledgments

We wish to acknowledge Pinellas County Reading/Language Arts Supervisors, Lynn McKay and Pat Nelms and Pinellas Writing Project Coordinators, Mary Osborne and Janie Guilbault. They implemented the Pinellas County Writing Project, providing writing training and materials for kindergarten through fifth-grade teachers.

We wish to thank the many teachers who have visited our writing demonstration classrooms to observe writing workshop. Their questions and comments allow us endless opportunities for growth.

A debt of gratitude is owed to Mary and Janie, our mentors from whom we continue to learn and gain insight. We also acknowledge Cathy Torres of the Pinellas County Writing Project for opening the door of writing to primary teachers.

We thank Claudia Stewart, our former principal, and Patricia Huffman, our present principal, for enabling us to develop, implement, and maintain a school-wide writing curriculum.

Finally, we acknowledge the teachers of Curtis Fundamental Elementary who have contributed much time and effort in supporting our efforts to promote written communication skills and to guide students in discovering the writer within themselves.

To our students, we can't thank you enough for the gifts of words you have given us.

Table of Contents

Writing Process and Writing Workshop

This book addresses three important needs of teachers. First and most importantly, it provides teachers with a striking way to help their students see the reading-writing connection. When students view themselves as writers, they become actively involved with print and feel empowered to make a difference in their own written expression.

Secondly, these lessons address expository and narrative writing skills, the primary types of writing students will use for life-long written communication. Daily writing tasks which require relating and describing information and events, explaining events or steps in a logical order, and exploring solutions to problems are basic examples of narrative and expository writing. Using literature to model expository and narrative writing skills helps students recognize and then apply these skills in their own writing.

Third, we have shared writing lessons with teachers across a variety of settings: our classrooms and school, county workshops, and statewide conferences. All welcomed the lesson ideas and eagerly asked for more. This response told us that teachers need a simple but effective approach to help them teach target writing skills.

The Writing Process

The writing process is a series of steps an author moves through to complete a piece of writing. The steps include brainstorming, writing, revising, editing, and publishing. Although the process for a piece of writing may take a day for some students and a month for others, it is important that you and the students view writing as a process with a beginning and ending that all writers experience.

Consider the analogy of baking a cookie. You can read the recipe, get all the ingredients ready and put them in a bowl, but you don't have a cookie until the dough is placed in the oven and baked. You might put the dough in the freezer and wait for another day to bake it. But you don't have a finished cookie until you do. If you stop at mixing the ingredients in a bowl, you will have cookie dough, but not a completed cookie.

A writer can have an idea in mind and begin to write some of it on paper, but it isn't a completed piece of writing until all the steps of the writing process are followed. That isn't to say that a student might not choose to continue a piece of writing at any stage for various reasons. Perhaps the topic is one the author doesn't really know enough to write about, or the writer simply doesn't choose to publish it. A first grade, emergent writer often stops at the composing stage. Fourth grade, developing writers may be reluctant to revisit a first draft. Both are exercising their empowerment as writers, which it is acceptable as long as students understand that writing is a process, and their pieces are not complete.

Brainstorming

Students begin the writing process with brainstorming, a step that serves as a rehearsal to attaining focused, organized writing. Brainstorming allows writers to remember past moments, recollect memorable experiences, and use their imaginations. These often serve as the seeds for composing.

How do you as a teacher encourage these thoughts to develop on paper? An excellent way is to read quality literature and share discussions related to the character, events, or topic. Through these discussions, students relate personal experiences that may trigger a similar memory for another student. Jot lists allow students to write down one or two words or a list of words that remind them of possible writing topics.

When students realize they have experiences or knowledge to share that are similar to the published author, they are given a purpose to write. Once the writer has discovered a purpose for writing, they proceed to the composing stage.

Composing

After students have generated an idea to write about, they are ready to begin composing. Information that you provide at this stage greatly influences a young writer's decisions about their work in progress. Specific lessons on developing focus, support, organization, and conventions need to be modeled by the teacher.

The writing conference is another valuable technique that helps a young writer in the composition stage. This personal, one-on-one conversation between you and the student about a piece of writing provides an opportunity for the student to discuss the progress of the piece and to learn how to make decisions about further developing the writing.

As you listen, you guide the young writer gently by asking simple questions like, "What are you working on?"; "Have you thought about _____?"; "What will you do next?"; "What is your favorite part?"; "How can I help?" Gentle, open-ended probing helps students find answers and ideas which give them a direction for their work.

Student pieces will vary in length and sophistication depending on the student's development as a writer. For example, a kindergarten student may compose a piece about her dog that may have only five or six words. By saying to her, "Tell me more about your dog," you invite the student to tell you about the piece of writing. The student probably can tell you more information than she is able to write. Depending on her development, you either can write the words for the student, or suggest that she add to the piece herself.

On the other hand, an intermediate student may write a full sheet of paper about her dog. By asking her, "What is the most important thing you want to share about your dog?" you help the student make decisions about the focus of her piece, as well as where to add further elaboration.

Composing may take one day or one week, depending on the skill development of the writer and the topic. The important result of this stage is that students effectively record their messages. They should feel confident that what is written on paper is the beginning of their own creations, generated by their own thinking.

Revision

The first draft is exactly that — the first time a student completes a piece of writing. It emerges from all the hard work the author demonstrated in the brainstorming and composing stages. The writing, however, is not finished.

Be careful not to imply that the first draft isn't good, or that more is better. Students often incorrectly assume that the more they write, the more meaningful the message. In reality, they probably have repeated themselves many times just to take up space on the paper.

We tell our students that writers are like artists. Instead of creating with clay or paint, they are crafting with words. Revision provides the opportunity to refine the writing. Students make choices about the clarity of writing at this stage.

Direct skill instruction and conferencing should demonstrate how to provide a tighter focus, improve a beginning or ending, add elaboration, or organize differently to make the piece flow more smoothly. Some conferencing questions that aid in the revision stage are "What did you mean by the word _____?"; "Do you see any verbs that you used over and over again?"; "Do you see any transition words that tell what happened first, second or last?"

Editing

Editing makes a written message crystal clear. Though you should not expect every piece of writing to be letter-perfect, you should tell students that attending to the details of a piece polishes it to a shine. Skill instruction at this stage should focus on complete sentences, correct punctuation, grammar, and spelling. Teaching editing symbols, such as carets for inserting words, or slashing letters to represent the need for capitals, is appropriate and useful.

Address spelling in the editing stage. Your expectations for spelling competency should match the developmental level of the student. For example, a first grader experimenting with word choice might use the word *tremendous* to describe his trip to the circus. Unless you are dealing with a child prodigy, don't expect *tremendous* to be spelled correctly. A fourth grader who attempts to use the same word and realizes it is spelled incorrectly should be expected to use the dictionary to find the correct spelling. Hold primary and intermediate grade students accountable for spelling basic sight words correctly, as well as those words that are posted in the classroom.

Publishing

Publishing allows students to feel proud of the work they have completed, and it gives them a chance to share it. You can publish the pieces in a variety of formal or informal ways. You can type them, or ask students to type them, on a computer or typewriter; bind them into a book; place them on posters, read them into a tape recorder; or ask students to rewrite them neatly on notebook paper. Not every piece of writing should be published, but students should understand and experience the complete writing process for at least some of their works.

When you give students the opportunity to practice the writing process, they feel a real sense of accomplishment when the piece of writing reaches the publishing stage. You will find that the writing process allows the writer to choose a personal goal and monitor progress toward that goal each day. Every student will not be at the same stage of writing on any given day. A student moves at a unique, personal rate supported by direct skill instruction, time to write, and teacher conferences.

Writing Workshop

Writing workshop teaches the writing process. It consists of three segments: a beginning mini-lesson, quiet writing and conferencing, and an ending sharing time. An entire writing workshop lasts from 30 to 45 minutes in the primary grades and 45 minutes to an hour in the intermediate grades.

The success of writing workshop depends on your ability to provide time for all three segments each day. Donald Graves, the father of writing workshop, stresses that writing must be practiced every day or its meaning will be lost.

> In short, it is extremely inefficient to miss a day...as our data on children show, when writers write every day, they begin to compose even when they are not composing. They enter into a 'constant state of composition'....If students are not engaged in writing at least four days out of five, and for a period of thirty-five to forty minutes, beginning in first grade, they will have little opportunity to learn to think through the medium of writing. When a teacher asks me, "I can only teach writing one day a week. What kind of program should I have?" my response is, "Don't teach it at all. You will encourage poor habits in your students and they will only learn to dislike writing. Think of something you enjoy doing well; chances are you involve yourself in it far more than one or two times a week. (Graves, p. 104, *Writing: Teachers and Children at Work.*)

The saying, "Practice makes perfect" applies to writing just as it does with any other interest, craft, or skill.

Mini-lessons for Skill Instruction

Writing workshop begins with a mini-lesson. A mini-lesson may be only a few minutes long, or it may be a more formal lesson of 20 to 30 minutes. More than one day may be required to complete a mini-lesson.

Think about the needs of the students as you prepare for a mini-lesson. Do the students need help in developing topics to write about? Are they struggling with focusing on a topic? Do they need to see how effective details can be to create meaningful messages for the reader? Do the students have bits of ideas scattered through their pieces and need help organizing one idea at a time? The answers to these questions will help you choose the specific lessons that will meet the needs of your students.

Include the basics of any other curriculum lesson as you develop the writing mini-lesson. Spend time building background before introducing the skill. Model the skill, and ask the students to practice it themselves. This book uses children's literature as a main model for writing skill instruction, and it provides a rich resource indeed.

Quiet Writing/Conferencing

Follow the mini-lesson with quiet writing and conferencing time. In the early part of the school year, this part of the workshop may be only five to ten minutes long, depending on the maturity of the students. Kindergarten students may write for five minutes; fourth graders for ten. As the students develop their writing skills, you should increase the writing time to fifteen minutes for kindergartners and 20 to 25 minutes for fourth and fifth graders. Short periods of writing time mean that students may not be able to finish their pieces, but that's fine. They will be eager to start the next day. You may find, as we have, that your students will beg for more time to write!

It is unfair to expect emerging writers in the primary grades to practice only the new skill that you present during the day's mini-lesson. When primary students listen daily to the same writers' language, engage in conversations using the vocabulary of writers, and read models of quality writing, they will begin naturally to use the instructed skills in their own pieces. Whatever the goal for any particular day, remember to spend time modeling the expected skill and behavior that you expect students to demonstrate during quiet writing time.

Students enter the intermediate grades as maturing writers. With a repertoire of writing experiences and a familiarity with writers' language, they are ready to further develop specific writing skills. At this stage of their development, students often use quiet writing time to practice the specific skill you present during instruction.

Students often use this time to choose whether they would like to begin new pieces or continue older pieces of writing. Writing workshop fosters a continual rehearsal for writing. The more often students write the more often they think about their writing outside of school. They tend to discuss their current works during the afternoon ride home or at the dinner table at night.

Quiet writing time requires students to incorporate all the skills they have acquired previously and to sharpen specific new skills besides. Actively take part in the quiet writing time yourself. When students see you using the time to practice writing, it sends the message that writing is a lifelong process of growth. As you practice writing with your students, you grow as a writer, too. When you allow yourself to grow as a writer, you become a better teacher of writing.

After writing for several minutes with your students, you should begin to circulate around the classroom to begin conferencing. Students see that their progress is important and that you are accessible. Keep a record of student conferences to help you keep track of who you have seen. You may wish to divide the class in sections and confer with a certain section each day. Having a sign up sheet for students to tell you when they need a conference is another way of setting up your conferencing. However you arrange it, set a goal to conference with each child once a week. The conference offers you an informal way to assess the progress of each writer and to collect information to share with parents.

Sharing

Invite students to share their pieces with the class during the last five to ten minutes of writing workshop. Keep track of those who have shared, just as you do with conferencing. Encourage each student to share at least once a week.

Sharing time is critical. The writer receives questions or comments about the piece. The listeners direct questions for clarification on any part of the piece, and offer comments about effective devices. The writers confirms the message and receives help about what to work on next.

Sharing also allows you to reinforce that day's mini-lesson, or perhaps a previous lesson, using the class as peer tutors. Responses from the students provide the teachable moments called *back door teaching*. If a student uses a strong lead, use the opportunity to point it out to the class. If a conference leads a student to add a specific describing word, sharing gives a chance to ask the student to explain why the word was changed.

Sharing teaches the class how to ask questions and share comments with the writer. At the same time, students make connections between the writer's piece and their own pieces, the writer's thinking and their own thinking.

Sharing is the essence of what author Lucy Calkins meant when she discussed the community of writers. It is a risky thing to share a piece of writing that represents a part of you. Students must feel that it is safe to share with their classmates.

You can help students feel comfortable with sharing. First, don't require that a student stand in front of the room when reading a piece. Some students feel more relaxed if they read their pieces from their seats, then stand as they receive comments. When you encourage writers to direct their voices toward the class, writers get the message that they have something important to share.

Secondly, you will need to model how to ask questions and how to share comments in a positive way. In the beginning of the year, students may be reluctant to share, feeling unsure that their writing will be accepted by their peers. Sharing your own pieces first is a wonderful way to break the ice. After you share, ask the students if they have any questions about your piece. Tell them that questions help a writer know which parts of the message are not clear enough.

Model appropriate, open-ended questions. For example, "Could you explain what you meant when...?" is much more appropriate than the question "Why did you use the word...which didn't make any sense?"

Next, invite students to share comments about pieces of writing. A typical comment from a student is, "I liked the whole thing." You can say, though, that a writer needs to know specifically what was effective and meaningful in a piece. Instruct students how to ask comments to elicit specifics, such as, "What part did you especially like?"

Model the difference between a positive and negative comment. An example of a positive comment that helps a writer improve is "I enjoyed listening to the funny part you said about your sister," or "I like the way you ended your piece." An offensive, and ultimately, damaging comment might be something like "I don't like pizza, so I wish you had written about some other kind of food." Create an enthusiastic atmosphere in the classroom, and it won't be long before everyone will want to share!

Teaching writing skills using children's literature is an effective and enjoyable way to incorporate the three components of writing workshop. If you practice writing workshop using children's literature to model specific writing skills for instruction, you have a valuable tool that helps develop eager and proficient writers.

You can use children's literature to teach brainstorming, focus, elaboration, organization, and convention skills. Students and teachers that we have worked with personally embrace the concept enthusiastically. They told us how much they would benefit from a collection of lessons. The result is this book.

How To Use This Book

Using Literature to Teach Writing

There has been a revolution in the teaching of writing at the elementary school level. Most states now require tests to assess student writing at particular grade levels. The tests are stringent and require that students master many skills to develop a complete piece of writing. Applying the writing process is necessary to fulfill these test requirements, as well as other academic and personal writing tasks.

These skills do not develop overnight. If students are to become successful writers — whether to achieve mastery of skills for their personal achievement and expression or to pass a test — writing instruction must begin in kindergarten. Classroom teachers must look at writing instruction with two goals in mind. First, they must guide students to view writing as a process which has a beginning and an end. Every step of the process emerges from thinking and planning. Secondly, teachers must look at writing instruction as a developmental continuum, moving students from understanding basic concepts of print to writing a focused, elaborated piece with a beginning, middle, and end.

As a teacher, you must provide the conditions in which students can learn to write. The task is not easy. Young writers must be given direct instruction in writing skills. They must see the skill modeled. They have to hear what the skill sounds like in a good piece of writing. Finally, they need time to practice the skill and share what they have written. These are the components of the daily writing workshop.

Children's literature provides a springboard to teach writing skills. Through literature students are able to see and hear quality writing. As you read aloud *Charlotte's Web* or *The Lion, the Witch, and the Wardrobe*, you have probably thought to yourself, "What incredible language!" These authors are masters of words. It seems only fitting that you would use their words to teach budding writers what excellence in writing can look and sound like. They in turn, will attempt these techniques in their own writing.

This book uses 20 different literature titles to teach specific expository and narrative writing skills. Expository writing explains information about a topic through descriptions, reasons, or steps. Narrative writing relates a fictional or non-fictional event through time. Fictional narratives include a setting, characters, and a plot. Both types of writing span the grade levels and require training to reach mastery. Literature can teach the skills needed for both genres.

We chose skills taken from our district's writing continuum, which is based on Florida's definition of effective writing. While the standards of other states and districts may vary slightly, the goal among them remains the same: that students should be able to produce a focused, well-supported and organized piece clearly written according to the conventions of English.

Target Skills for Primary and Intermediate Students

All writers need direct instruction in the areas of content, organization, and conventions. The skills in this book are chosen because they are significant in the development of a mature writer. The introductory page for each target skill group provides background information for you and suggests alternative literature for teaching the same skill. Realize that many students will not grasp the target skill the first time it is introduced and will require more practice.

Although the lessons in the book are divided into primary and intermediate sections, the age of the student writers are not as important as the level of their mastery of the skill. Think of the labels *primary* and *intermediate* as tags to distinguish the complexity of the lesson, not necessarily to serve as a grade level barrier. Primary lessons introduce a skill, while the intermediate lesson reviews and refines it.

A high-functioning primary class may benefit from moving on to the intermediate lesson, while intermediate students struggling with the skill of varied sentence structure profit from trying the primary lesson first. Teachers of exceptional-education students may choose to use parts of either a primary or intermediate lesson to introduce a skill to their students and should adapt the lessons to suit the needs of their students.

Since students must realize that all writing is the result of thinking, and thinking takes time, the skill of brainstorming is listed first. Brainstorming allows students to view themselves as writers when they discover the amazing connection between the experiences in their lives to the characters and topics represented in published literature. The literature books chosen provide a model for techniques to teach this skill. The use of jot lists and story planners helps students rehearse their writing.

Once students have decided what to write about, they need to practice required skills to focus on their topic. Not straying from a topic is a difficult task. The children's literature found in this section are examples of writing that remains focused on a clearly defined topic from the beginning of the book to the end. Allowing students to listen to and read published pieces of writing, especially those having to do with a topic they enjoy, encourages them to attempt the skill of focus in their own writing. This is authentic learning!

After students are able to write several meaningful sentences about one topic they are ready to learn elaboration skills. Children's books are filled with elaboration techniques such as alliteration, metaphor, simile, onomatopoeia, and descriptive language. Elaborative writing takes effort and skills, but the result is rich language that is fun to listen to and to read. If you introduce these skills, model them with the literature suggested in this book, and give students many opportunities to practice, their writing will knock your socks off!

The children's literature chosen for this section provides wonderful examples of elaboration. Your students may already be familiar with some of these books. This is good because quality children's literature should be revisited more than once. A truly good book holds within its covers many lessons. The lessons in this section build on one another. Because of that, we suggest that you present them in the order given.

As students begin to put more words on paper, and those words begin to grow into sentences, organization becomes an issue. It doesn't matter how focused and elaborated a story is if the information is scattered. Bits and pieces of ideas make it difficult for the reader to make connections and to gather meaning from the writing. We have included two books in this section, but most well-written children's books adapt themselves to teaching this skill.

Students develop the concept of organization by listening to literature such as fairy tales, which have a clear beginning, middle, and end. By internalizing the structure of complete stories they are able to apply the required beginning, middle, and end in their own pieces. As students compose their own organized pieces, they will be ready to learn the value of transition words. Effective use of transition words clearly defines the organization of a piece and allows the meaning to flow smoothly.

The final section of lessons concerns the conventions of language. Recording events on paper is valuable only if it can be understood by others who read it. Many words and punctuation marks in the English language serve specific functions. Young writers must understand what these words and marks are and know how to use them appropriately. They learn that through practice.

We included these writing skills last because they are the most complex. Identifying and using active verbs is not an easy assignment. Using a varied sentence structure in a piece of writing does not come effortlessly for most writers. Young writers must recognize the value of conversation in writing before they will attempt it in their own writing.

As a teacher, you are the best judge of which writing skills are developmentally appropriate for your students. Students who have been immersed in reading and writing and given ample time to practice all the skills introduced up to this point, however, will welcome the opportunity to try something new.

Format of Mini-lessons

These lessons contain the three components of writing workshop. The title of the literature selection and the level of the lesson is stated first. Next are the materials you need to assemble before the lesson and the target skill.

The mini-lesson itself is organized as follows. The Build Background portion of the mini-lesson prepares students for the literature to be shared. It also sets the stage for teaching students how to think and speak like a writer. You then read the book aloud and model the target skill. Time near the end of the mini-lesson gives students an opportunity to practice the skill with the support of the teacher and the class. Finally, students move to a quiet writing area to practice the skill alone.

When Quiet Writing/Conferencing time occurs every day, its effectiveness is enhanced. Provide students with a folder or portfolio to hold their pieces. Saving pieces from previous writing workshops allows all students choice and room to grow as writers. Students may want to revise or edit previous pieces using the target skill from that particular day's mini-lesson. Hearing a lead they like in a literature book might prompt them to try the same type of lead in older pieces. Keep in mind that younger writers frequently start a new piece each day. They might not even practice the target skill on the day you introduce it.

The sharing portion of these lessons will be different in any given classroom because the nature of each class is special. Time usually allows for three to five students to share their writing for the day. Many teachers use a special chair or stool for the writer, and the rest of the class becomes the audience. This time allows students to hear the target skill used within the context of a writing piece. We do not include questions under the sharing section of each lesson because they are most meaningful when they come from within the context of the classroom. You may wish, however, to refer to the sharing questions suggested throughout the section on writing workshop.

The Issue of Time

Can writing workshop be practiced every day? The time dilemma usually rears its ugly head when the subject of the practicality of a daily writing workshop comes up. The issue of time versus curriculum requirements is a familiar one to all teachers, regardless of grade level. Using literature books to teach writing skills is one way to solve this dilemma. Use literature to instruct writing skills, and integration of the curriculum is made simpler. A primary teacher can combine shared reading, phonics instruction, and writing instruction together into one block of time. An intermediate teacher can review a language skill before the reading of the literature book and then make note of how it was used in the context of the book. The application of these skills in context, rather than in isolated practice, often proves more valuable. At every level, content areas may be integrated with writing instruction by reading a non-fiction book such as *A Walk in the Rainforest*.

Closing Thoughts

The wealth of children's literature books grows each day. Hearing a great story is a treat no matter what your age! At our fingertips is the secret for helping our students become successful writers. The secret is waiting in your library.

This collection of mini-lessons should not be used as an entire curriculum, but rather as a supplement. We recommend these books to you as authentic models from which to teach writing skills. Writing similes as eloquently as Jane Yolen in *Owl Moon* or descriptive language as beautiful as Angela Johnson's doesn't just happen from sharing these books with children. Allowing students to see and hear quality literature, however, enhances their ability to recognize and develop clear, focused, and elaborated language in their own pieces. By using these lessons, you can guide your students into being as proficient in these skills as the authors they love to listen to. Authentic models lead to authentic learning.

All of the books in this collection may be used for more than one writing skill lesson. For example, *Bigmama's* by Donald Crews could be used for a lesson in brainstorming as well as the lesson on prepositions included here. *The Important Book* by Margaret Wise Brown provides an incredible model for the use of details, as well as focus. We encourage you to revisit all the books. Let these books become as comfy as Ira's much-loved teddy.

We hope you enjoy using this collection of mini-lessons. But more than that, we know through our own experience that you and your students will share bountiful gifts of words as they learn to write from listening to a good book.

CHAPTER ONE

Brainstorming

The first section of mini-lessons addresses the pre-writing stage of the writing process. The goal is to show student writers that they already hold a wealth of stories and writing topics in their heads. The events that make up their own individuality are worthy to write about. When a first grader rushes into the classroom eager to tell you about the loss of a first tooth, the connection needs to be made that the first lost tooth is a story waiting to be written down. A visit to grandma's house on an airplane is the seed for a terrific piece of writing. When students are vested in their own writing, it belongs to them, and it begins to matter to them that their ideas transform into words.

Brainstorming, or pre-writing, may take the form of pictures, surveys, or conversations. The jot list often is used to make a quick list of notes, ideas, or possible topics to write about. You will know your students are pre-writing when they discuss events in their lives as possible writing topics. A second grader might say, "On my way to school I was thinking about what I was going to write about today, and I can't decide whether to write about the new pair of shoes I got or that my cat ate a lizard." A fourth grader may check his brainstorm list for a new topic and decide to start a piece about his favorite place. Both children view their lives as worthy of recording in print.

For both primary and intermediate grades, it is worthwhile to have an ongoing personal list of topics for students to write about. In the primary grades this may be a posted list of topics such as family, pets, and trips. The students will personalize the topic when given the opportunity to write. By the time students are in third grade they may keep ongoing personal lists of topics to write about in their writing folders. Encourage students to add new ideas to the list frequently. This enables young writers to keep topics to write about at their fingertips rather than spend time thinking or telling the teacher, "I don't know what to write about."

Story telling is an important part of any culture. In the book, *Tell Me A Story, Mama*, students hear one child's memory of stories told to her by her own mother when she was small. They in turn may remember stories they have been told by their parents or other relatives. Leading students to see the importance of recording these stories so they can be told over and over gives them a purpose for writing. Emergent, developing, and mature writers write best when they write about what they know.

When I Was Little initiates conversation between students about many of the events that happened to them when they were four years old. Thinking about and talking about topics enables young writers to organize and rehearse their thoughts first. Only then can they turn their thoughts into the written word.

When I Was Young in the Mountains captures mountain life in the past. The little girl who tells the story loved being in the mountains so much that she knew she would never leave. As students hear about her memories they are drawn into thinking about places which have given them wonderful memories, too.

Expository and narrative text that allows all students to choose their own topics results in writing pieces that are meaningful and worthwhile to the author. Literature often provides the nudge to finding a purpose for writing.

Two other pieces of literature to use for developing brainstorming are:

Wilfred Gordon McDonald Partridge by Mem Fox
When the Relatives Came by Cynthia Rylant

When I Was Young in the Mountains

by Cynthia Rylant

Primary Lesson

Materials:

When I Was Young in the Mountains, a large United States map, two large pieces of lined chart paper, one piece of lined paper cut in half vertically for each student, dark marker, writing folders or notebooks, paper, pencils

Mini-lesson:

brainstorming ideas to write about

Mini-lesson

A. Build background.

Show a map of the United States. Name your state and find it on the map.

Ask if all children in the United States were born in your state. (No, they weren't.)

Ask for students who were born in another state besides the one they are currently living in to raise their hand.

Point out that even though some of the class was born in other states, right now all of the students are living in the same state found on the big map of the United States. Mention that because the students in the class do live in the same state, there are activities they probably do that are similar. Children who live in a mountain state probably go snow skiing in the winter. Children who live near a lake or a river probably go fishing. Children who live near the ocean probably go to the beach. Children everywhere have fun activities that they like to do.

B. Introduce the book and the author.

Tell the class the book is about all the fun activities a little girl remembers from growing up in the state of Tennessee. Have the class listen for these activities as the book is read.

C. Read the book aloud.

D. Discuss the following.

Ask for volunteers to share activities the young girl experienced in the story. On a large sheet of chart paper, record their responses. When completed, the chart will look like the chart labeled Chart One, found after the sharing portion of this lesson.

Tell the class that they have just discovered the brainstorming list for the little girl in the book. Each one of the memories recorded on the chart paper is a special time the little girl remembered and one she could write about.

Explain that a brainstorming list holds ideas authors know a lot about such as something that has either happened to them or something they are good at doing. It could be a list of favorite toys, special places, memories, or special activities that are really fun to play.

Tell students that if an author is looking for an idea to write about, he or she could look at a brainstorming list and find a topic waiting there. The teacher should note topics will lend themselves to either expository or narrative writing. Help students to know which type of pieces they are writing. If they are explaining how or why about their topic, it is an expository piece. If they are telling a story about an event that has happened to them, it is a narrative piece.

E. **Model the skill.**

Place a clean sheet of chart paper where all students can see it clearly. Tell the class they are going to do a group brainstorming list. Explain that means fun activities the class agrees upon are going to be written on the chart as a possible writing topic. They need to get so many ideas going inside their brains that it causes a storm of topics to flow out.

At the top of the chart print the words *brainstorm list*. Going down the side of the page, number from one to five.

Next, ask a volunteer to share an activity he or she likes to do. Ask for a show of hands who also like to do that activity. If most students agree, write that activity on the brainstorm chart. For example, if the activity mentioned was swimming at the beach, the teacher would write *swimming at the beach* on the chart.

Continue this pattern with students naming an activity, the class voting by show of hands if they want it on the list, and then writing it. When the chart has five items listed, reread them together. See Chart Two for an example.

Tell the class that they can now use the brainstorming list to find a writing topic.

Give each student a piece of paper. Have them choose one topic from the brainstorming list and write it at the top of the paper. The teacher should model with the class, writing a topic on a piece of chart paper or on the overhead.

Ask students to think about what they know about the topic they have chosen. Explain those are the words or sentences they need to write down.

The teacher again should model how to write a few words or sentences about the chosen topic.

The teacher can help students in getting their thoughts on paper by segmenting sounds for emergent writers or asking early writers to tell you more.

Quiet Writing/Conferencing

As students move into independent, quiet writing ask them to write either more words or more sentences about their chosen topics, according to their developmental level. As you conference with students, encourage them to make lists of everything they know about the topics. They should be saved in the students' writing folders. These lists can be composed into more developed pieces during future writing workshops.

Sharing

Choose three students to share the words or sentences they have written using a single topic chosen from the brainstorm list. Ask the students how the brainstorm lists helped them get their writing pieces started. Students can add topics to the list as they discover other similar interests. Refer students to the brainstorm list if they have difficulty deciding on topics to write about.

Charts

Primary Lesson
for
When I Was Young in the Mountains

Chart One

1. Grandfather coming home
2. Grandmother's cooking
3. Eating too much
4. The swimming hole
5. Mr. and Mrs. Crawford
6. Baths
7. Church
8. Sounds
9. Snake
10. Swing

Chart Two

Example of a Group Brainstorm List

1. Swimming in the ocean
2. Playing soccer
3. Eating ice cream
4. Playing with my friends
5. Going on vacation

When I Was Young in the Mountains

by Cynthia Rylant

Intermediate Lesson

Materials:

When I Was Young in the Mountains, chart paper, markers, students' notebooks and writing folders

Mini-lesson:

brainstorming ideas to write about

Mini-lesson

A. Build background.

Ask students if they have ever been to places that they never wanted to leave. The special place may be close by or far away; they may visit them often or only once in awhile. Invite a few kids to share just the names of the special places.

Now ask students if they know the meaning of *contentment.* Discuss this word, and relate it to being in a place where a person feels so comfortable that she is happy enough to stay there forever.

Ask students to think about what kinds of things make them feel comfortable in their special places.

B. Introduce book and author.

Tell students to look for the things that made the girl love the mountains.

C. Read book aloud.

D. Discuss the following.

Ask students what kinds of things made the girl feel content in the mountains. Make a list similar to Chart One which follows the Sharing portion of the lesson.

Ask students how Cynthia Rylant shows the reader that the little girl loved being in the mountains so much.

Model with the students how to brainstorm a list of places you (the teacher), feel comfortable being in or visiting. Then develop a list of things that make that place so special to you. See Chart Two. Explain to students that the term *brainstorm* describes these lists because their brains are having storms of ideas. To keep track of them and be able to look at them later, they need to write down the brainstorming ideas.

Quiet Writing/Conferencing

Ask students to think about special places they have visited. Have them choose their topics and brainstorm lists of items that make those places so special. Students may then begin writing in detail about each item on their personal lists to develop a description of their special places. Remind students that this type of writing is expository because they are describing a topic.

You may also have students write narratives about times they visited their special places for a future writing workshop.

Sharing

Before each student shares a piece, ask what part of Cynthia Rylant's book reminded the writer of each personal topic. After each student shares, model how to ask effective questions of the writer and how to offer valuable comments. Invite the students to do the same. Tell students to keep their pieces in their writing folders.

Charts

Intermediate Lesson
for
When I Was Young in the Mountains

Chart One

What did the girl love about being in the mountains?

waiting for Grandfather to come home from work
eating special foods that Grandmother made
using the johnny-house in the middle of the night
walking through the cow pasture and woods
playing in the swimming hole
visiting the general store
pumping water from the well
drinking hot chocolate
going to church
watching baptisms in the swimming hole
listening to and seeing wildlife
having a funny picture taken
sharing quiet times on the porch

Chart Two

Sample Brainstorming List for Intermediate Lesson

My list of special places

my backyard
my apartment building
the beach
a mountain forest
my family room
church
the neighborhood I live in

Topic: a mountain forest

seeing all the different evergreen trees
smelling the scent of the pine needles
watching wildlife such as hawks, owls, eagles, deer
hearing waterfalls and rushing creeks
eating lunch on a boulder in the middle of a creek
stretching my legs over fallen tree trunks
searching for trail markers
following winding paths up mountain trails
listening to peace

When I Was Little

by Jamie Lee Curtis

Primary Lesson

Materials:

When I Was Little, one piece of large lined chart paper, lined paper and pencil for every student, writing folders or notebooks, marker

Mini-lesson:

brainstorming ideas to write about

Mini-lesson

A. Build background.

Have students who remember what they did on their last birthday raise their hands. Ask one or two of those students to share.

Have students who have a memory of a visit to someone special this year raise their hands. Ask one or two of those students to share.

Have students who remember playing a sport to raise their hands. Ask one or two of those students to share.

Note aloud that the class seems to have a lot of memories about many different things.

B. Introduce the book and the author.

Explain that the author wrote the book with the help of her daughter, Annie. Show the cover of the book and point out Annie.

Explain that the book is a collection of memories that Annie has of when she was a baby. Note that she is making new memories at her current age of four years old.

Ask the class to listen for those memories as the book is read.

C. Read the book aloud.

D. Discuss the following.

Ask for volunteers to recount Annie's memories. As the class reviews the highlights of the book, write the highlights on a large sheet of chart paper. The chart should resemble the chart labeled Chart One found after the Sharing section of this lesson.

When you finish the review, reread the chart with the students. Explain that each memory that Annie wrote about in the book is a special topic. Annie could probably tell us more about when she painted her toenails bubble-gum pink or where she was going in the car every day when she waved at the policeman, but she didn't.

Point out that each item on the chart list could be a separate topic for Annie to write more about. She has a special memory of each and could probably write a separate story about each. This chart list could be a list of writing topics just for Annie.

E. **Model the skill.**

Ask students to think back to the memories they shared with the class in the Building Background section of the lesson.

Knowledge of a sport, a special birthday, or a visit to someone special would all be topics they could use for a piece of writing. Assure them that the stories in their heads belong only to them. That is why authors often make their own private lists of topics to write about, called a brainstorm list.

Place a large sheet of chart paper where all students can see it clearly. Then pass out a lined sheet of paper to every student. For emergent writers, have the title *Things I Can Write About* pre-printed at the top of their paper. For developing writers, simply model on the chart paper where to place the heading, *Things I Can Write About.*

Explain that they will make their own personal brainstorm list.

Return to the topics mentioned previously: sports, birthdays, and special visits. Ask for volunteers to name a few sports. Examples might be baseball, gymnastics, soccer, or swimming.

On the chart paper, write the word *sports*. Underneath sports, write all the examples the students gave. The chart should look similar to Chart Two found behind the Sharing section of this lesson. Instruct students to choose a sport they know something about.

Write the name of that sport on the first line of their paper.

Explain this is now a topic they could write about during writing workshop.

Have all students write the word *birthday* on line two of their papers. The teacher should write *birthday* on the large chart as well. Tell the students that everyone has a birthday to celebrate in their own special way. Because birthdays are fun to write and read about, a birthday makes a great topic for a writing piece.

Finally, write *special visit* on the third line of the chart. Ask for volunteers to name people they have visited. List a few responses on the chart paper.

Tell the students to pick one or two of those special people and write their names on their piece of paper. Explain that they have just started a list of writing topics. Often a writer gets stuck and can't think of a thing to write about. Special lists of words like this brainstorm list can help remind students of a topic so they can get started writing.

Quiet Writing/Conferencing

The teacher should choose a topic from the list. Use a think-aloud technique, telling the class how that particular word reminded you of a topic to write about. To help them get started, model a few sentences about that topic.

Instruct students to choose topics from their own personal lists and begin writing. Emergent writers may write lists of words that go with the topic. Developing writers may write several sentences. Both are acceptable as they are writing what they know at their own developmental level. Narrative writing at these levels may take the form of retelling the special visit. Expository writing would be choosing a favorite sport from the topic list and explaining how to play it.

Sharing

Choose three students to share a piece of writing they worked on during writing workshop. Ask which word from their personal lists helped them choose topics. Although they may respond with only a few words or a few sentences, ask the audience if the author's piece reminded them of a similar topic they might want to write about. Encourage students to piggyback each other's topics. Using the teacher chart, model how to add topics to the list.

Charts

Primary Lesson
for
When I Was Little

Chart One

The charts that the students generate will not have all of these memories listed. Feel free to add any yourself. This activity helps students note all the different writing topics Annie could use that are found in her own life.

Cried a lot	Songs
Silly hair	Swim in the pool
Painted my toenails	Park
Spilled a lot	Granny
Waved at policemen	Food
Mommy and Me	Tickle torture
Nursery school	Family
Time-outs	

Chart Two

Student/Teacher-modeled Brainstorm List

SPORTS
(Students choose one of these topics to write on their list.)

baseball
football
gymnastics
swimming
soccer
ice skating

BIRTHDAY
SPECIAL VISIT
(Students choose one or two of these people to place on their topic lists as potential topics.)

Grandma
Aunt
Friend
Cousin

When I Was Little

by Jamie Lee Curtis

Intermediate Lesson

Materials:

When I Was Little, chart paper, markers, students' notebooks and writing folders

Mini-lesson:

brainstorming ideas to write about

Mini-lesson

A. Build background.

Ask students, *If someone asked you to describe yourself what would you say?* Share a few responses.

Ask students to think about some of the ways they are the same and some of the ways they are different now compared to when they were four years old. Have them share a few differences.

Ask students what kinds of things may change about them in the next ten years. Share a few responses.

Tell students that when we are able to see changes and growth in ourselves we are able to describe who we are as individual people. We may be the same as others in some ways, but different in other ways.

B. Introduce book and author.

Tell students that as you read this book aloud they should think about what has changed in their lives in the last few years.

C. Read book aloud.

D. Discuss the following.

Ask students to recall some of the changes the little girl saw in herself from the time when she was four years old. Make a jot list of these changes on chart paper. See sample chart which follows the Sharing portion.

Review each change and have students describe how that item has changed in their lives. Share one or two for each item.

Reread the second-to-last page of the book and discuss. Ask students to brainstorm other areas of life that affect who they are. See the chart for examples.

Quiet Writing/Conferencing

Ask students to write a list of words that describe themselves. Explain that this list is called a jot *list* because they will be jotting down possible ideas to write about. A jot list is used to record thoughts and ideas writers think about or brainstorm. They may want to use the chart as a starting place, but they should not limit themselves to those items. Each student should choose one or two ideas to write about.

Tell students that this type of writing may be expository or narrative. Consider the following example on the topic of *What I am allowed to do*. Students may describe certain television programs they may watch, how far they are allowed to ride their bicycles, or when they are permitted to play with friends. Explain that this type of writing is expository writing because the writer is explaining something about the topic. However, students may choose to write short narratives about the same topics. Examples may be a short story relating a time when friends came over, or a time when they rode their bicycles too far from home, relating the consequences which followed. Explain that this type of writing is narrative writing because events move forward in time.

Sharing

Before each student shares a piece, ask which topic was chosen. In addition, ask the student if the piece describes the topic and is expository writing or if the piece tells a story and is narrative writing. After each student shares a piece, model how to ask questions of the writer and how to offer comments. Invite the other students to do the same. Tell students to keep their jot lists and pieces of writing in their folders.

Chart

Intermediate Lesson
for
When I Was Little

What do I know about myself?

my physical size

how I communicate

being a boy or girl

how I wear my hair

what I am allowed to eat

what I am allowed to do

causing trouble or being helpful

how I do certain things

what kind of social or learning experiences I have had

getting punished

taking care of myself

Other items that affect who I am

who I live with

what I like to do in my spare time

things I am very good at doing

things I would like to do better

what I am interested in learning about

Tell Me A Story, Mama

by Angela Johnson

Primary Lesson

Materials:

Tell Me A Story, Mama, chart paper, marker, story planner worksheet for every student, transparency, transparency marker, paper, pencils, writing folders or notebooks

Mini-lesson:

brainstorming a topic

Mini-lesson

A. **Build background.**

Ask students if their parents have ever told them stories about when they were very young. Invite a few students to share. Explain that they also tell stories every day. When they rush into the classroom and tell a friend about the school roller skating party, that is telling a story. Whenever a tooth is lost or a birthday is celebrated, and they share what happened with someone else, that is telling a story. Everyone in the class is a storyteller.

B. **Introduce the book and the author.**

Tell the class that the book is a collection of stories a mother shares with her little girl. They are stories of when the mother was a little girl herself.

Ask them to listen for similar stories their mothers have ever told them, or if any of the events in the story have also happened to them.

C. **Read the story aloud. Note that Mama knew many stories.**

D. **Discuss the following.**

Ask the following questions.
What story did the mother tell about the mean old lady?
What story did the mother tell about the puppy?
What story did the mother tell about going on the train?

Explain that good storytellers remember to include a beginning, middle, and an end to their story. They also include details so the reader will get a clear picture of their story.

Ask the class if they thought the author was a good storyteller. Why or why not?

E. **Model the skill.**

Ask students to think about something that has recently happened to them. Maybe they recently had small injuries, or lost teeth, or went on overnight trips somewhere. These events will become their writing topics.

Show the transparency of the story planner found after the Sharing section of this lesson. Model how to fill out the first line that reads, *My story will be about _____.* Have students fill out their own sheets. Segment the sounds for emergent writers individually. Phonetic spelling is acceptable.

Move to the next section that reads, *Draw a Picture of the Setting*. Model with students how to fill in the box. Next, model how to fill out the *characters* section, including the illustration.

Finish with the problem and solution. For emergent writers, you will need to redefine what a problem and a solution are. These are terms they should be familiar with through shared-reading instruction.

Quiet Writing/Conferencing

Model with students how to turn their story planners into completed pieces of writing that tell their stories. This process will probably take more than one day. The first day's mini-lesson could be spent on filling in the planner itself. For the second day's lesson you could demonstrate how to use the planner to compose the piece.

Emergent and developing writers find it easier to compose a non-fiction narrative piece. Encourage students to write what they know about. A story planner is a great tool for planning a fictional narrative piece when the student is ready. Story planners can be developed by the teacher or found in commercial reading programs. These help students organize their thoughts to tell their individual stories.

Planners are a helpful tool to organize thoughts in expository pieces as well. Students can choose their topics of study and write three sentences about what they know. Then students can elaborate under each statement. See the Expository Planner following the Story Planner.

When students are having trouble deciding on writing topics, encourage them to think about stories they have told someone that day. Even if it was simply to say, *It is supposed to rain today*, help them to see that a rainy day would make an excellent topic for a piece of writing. Story planners then can help them get started to write.

Sharing

Choose three students to share their story planners and then their pieces aloud. When planners have been composed into narrative form, ask students to make note of sentences found in the planner that are also found in the narrative form. This will reinforce how important the planning stage of writing is.

When students begin to share their own experiences related to another student's topic, remind them that they could write pieces on those topics as well.

Story Planner

My story will be about _____

Draw a picture of the setting.

My characters are: _____

Draw a picture of the characters

Name: _____   Name: _____   Name: _____

Problem _____

Solution

Expository Planner

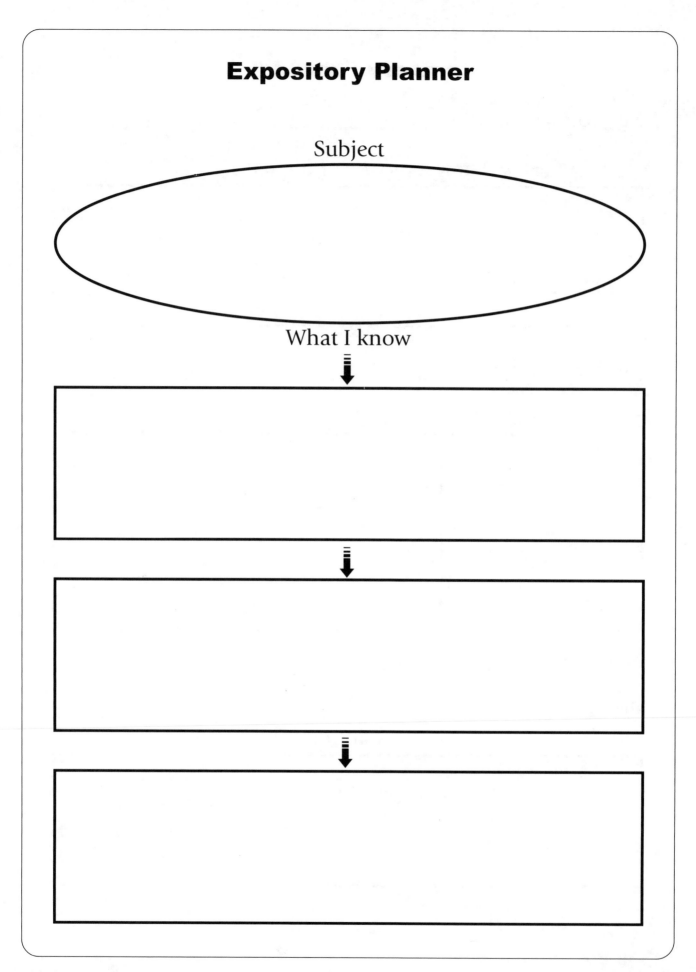

Subject

What I know

Tell Me a Story, Mama

by Angela Johnson

Intermediate Lesson

Materials:

Tell Me a Story, Mama, chart paper, markers, students' notebooks and writing folders

Mini-lesson:

brainstorming ideas to write about

Mini-lesson

A. Build background.

Ask students if they can remember special stories that have been passed down in their families: stories they have heard over and over again and probably have memorized. Have a few students share.

Ask students what makes these stories so special to them. Explain to students that the reason people like to remember these special stories and retell them is because they bring to life some important times that were happy, sad, or funny.

Tell students that the person telling the story must be a good storyteller if someone will want to hear a story again.

B. Introduce book and author.

Tell students that the mother in this book must have been a good storyteller because her daughter knows many stories by heart. Even though she has heard them many times, she wants to hear them again.

Tell students that as you read the book you need them to figure out who the real storyteller is. Ask them to notice if this book reminds them of similar stories in their own lives.

C. Read book aloud.

D. Discuss the following.

Ask students who they think took the part of the storyteller.

Ask students how they think the daughter was able to retell so many stories.

Ask students to remember and share some of the topics in the stories she told. Record these topics in a column on chart paper. (See sample which follows the Sharing portion of this lesson.)

As you review each topic, talk about the feelings that must have been involved with each story to make them so memorable.

Review each topic. This time, read each one aloud and have students jot down on their papers personal times that the topics help them remember. Give students a few minutes to think about and write about each one. While students are writing their topics, you may record yours as well on the chart paper or in your notebook. Then have two to three students share their personal topics. Jot down a few of their topics next to the author's topics on the chart paper. Giving students time to think, sharing some of their topics aloud, and recording some of their topics will help the other, more reluctant students with brainstorming.

As you conclude the lists of personal topics, tell students that they have just experienced what every writer has to do before writing, and that is called *brainstorming*. Explain that this term fits because their brains are having a storm of ideas. They don't want to lose the ideas, so it's important to jot them down.

Quiet Writing/Conferencing

Tell students that the type of writing which tells a story is called narrative writing. Ask students to choose one topic from their brainstorming list which they would like to begin writing a narrative piece about. After choosing their topics, students should make jot lists of the important ideas about their topics to help plan the writing. Then they may add details to the items on their lists to write their pieces. Keep in mind that it will take several days to complete these pieces of writing, following the steps of the writing process.

Sharing

Before each student shares a piece, ask which topic from the book reminded him of his personal topic. After a student reads a piece, model how to ask questions about the piece and how to offer comments on the piece. Invite the other students to do the same. Tell students to keep the brainstorm lists and pieces of writing in their writing folders for future writing workshops.

Chart

Intermediate Lesson
for
Tell Me A Story, Mama

Author's topic	Personal topic
throwing mud at a mean old lady's fence	the time my sister fell and cut her knee when mean, old Mr. Merusi chased the kids off his property
a loving Grandmama	my Uncle Gilbert helping me out during a difficult time
bringing home an orphaned puppy	how I found Cougar, Dixie & Gracee
being separated from parents; living with relatives	
spending time during summer with other relatives	vacation with Aunt Ronnie; spending a summer with Aunt Jane
crying when you feel like it	
best friend moved away	when I moved in 6th grade; moving from New Jersey to Florida
growing up and moving away from parents	my first apartment
	buying my first house
	plans to build a log cabin in North Carolina

CHAPTER TWO

Focus

Children often vacillate between one main idea and another while trying to find focus in their writing. Students need to understand that this is a normal part of the writing process. Through constant review and modeling, student writers will begin to recognize that there can be only one main topic that governs their pieces. Every time you say, *Tell me what you are writing about*, or *Tell me what you are reading about*, you provide practice in identifying focus.

Focus is a difficult skill, one that most emergent and early writers will not master. When young writers are asked what their piece is about, they will often retell the entire story. Leading them to recognize that the most important event will become the main idea of their story takes much practice. It also is difficult for emergent and early writers to realize that writing a lot about a topic isn't the best way to focus their writing.

On the other hand, suggesting that words or sentences should be taken out of a story can be devastating for any writer. Modeling how to delete unimportant information effectively will have to be repeated many times for most students.

Intermediate teachers need to explain and model the difference between writing that is focused and writing that is merely on-topic. Consider the following example. A student may be writing a narrative piece about a recent birthday party. The student may write about everything related to the party, from sending invitations, to shopping for the party supplies, then decorating the house, and finally having the party itself. Is this writing on the topic? Yes, but it is not focused. If the topic is the birthday party, then the focus needs to be the party, not everything leading up to the party. You will need to demonstrate such examples for their students to see the difference between writing that is on-topic and focused and writing that is on-topic but off-focus.

As the quiet writing portion of the writing workshop moves into conferencing, have student writers state what their pieces of writing are about before the conference begins. This form of practice will help students remain aware of their topics as they shape the piece.

Other books that may be used to model focus in writing:

The Quilt Story by Tony Johnston and Tomie dePaola
The Mitten by Jan Brett

The Big Block of Chocolate

by Janet Slater Redhead

Primary Lesson

Materials:

The Big Block of Chocolate, focused and unfocused photographs, chocolate bar, name cards for characters in the story (optional), chart of *The Circus*, colored marker, pencils, writing folders or notebooks, paper

Mini-lesson:

focus on a topic

Mini-lesson

A. Build background.

Show the class a photograph that was taken out of focus. Show them the same photograph taken in focus. Discuss the difference between the two pictures.

Lead them to determine that the out-of-focus picture is hard to see. It is fuzzy, and it is hard to tell the subject of the picture. But the focused picture is clear and easy to make out.

Explain that writing sometimes gets fuzzy if there are too many words or sentences that don't have anything to do with the story being told. It becomes hard to remember what the story is even about, just like the unfocused picture is hard to see.

B. Introduce the book and the author.

Ask students to predict what they think the book will be about.

Ask why no student predicted the story would be about a dinosaur or a big block of ice. The title indicates the story is about a big block of chocolate. If the author was writing a story about a dinosaur or a block of ice, the title would have been different. We know the focus of the story will be about a block of chocolate because the title says so.

C. Read the book aloud.

D. Discuss the following.

Ask if the class prediction was correct. Was the story about a big block of chocolate? Did the author mention a dinosaur or a big block of ice? No, the author remained focused on the topic, a big block of chocolate. The book wasn't fuzzy. It always was easy to determine the main idea of the story.

Even though the chocolate passed from Miss Jenny to the dog to the cat to the magpie to the ant, the focus remained on the big block of chocolate itself.

Students could even take on the roles of Miss Jenny and the animals and pass a bar of chocolate between them as in the book. After each pass, ask the students, *Where is your focus?* It is on the block of chocolate.

E. Model the skill.

Show Chart One found after the Sharing portion of this lesson. Read the title, *The Circus*. Ask students to predict what the story will be about.

Tell the students to listen as you read the paragraph aloud for any sentences that do not seem to be focused on the circus.

Instruct them to raise their index fingers each time they hear a sentence that does not belong in the story.

Next, ask for a volunteer to underline with a marker any sentence they heard that was unfocused. Kindergarten students can paraphrase a sentence out loud while the teacher underlines the unfocused sentence.

Explain that the underlined sentences should not be in the circus story because they have nothing to do with a circus.

Reread the paragraph without the underlined sentences so students can hear the difference.

Quiet Writing/Conferencing

Give each student a sentence strip. Have each student write one sentence that explains something that can be found in the classroom.

Then have students tape the sentence strips on the chalkboard or on an easel. Reread each sentence, and have the class decide whether it was focused on the topic of *things found in the classroom*. If the sentence is not focused, remove the strip from the chalkboard or easel.

Before moving to quiet, individual writing, have each student try to share in one or two words their topic for that day's writing workshop. Remind students to write only words or sentences that are focused on their topics.

Sharing

Choose three students to share their pieces of writing from the day's writing workshop. After each student has shared, have a volunteer state the focus of the piece. Have the author share whether the volunteer was correct. If the piece appeared to have any unfocused sentences, point them out to the author. Begin with, *I was a little confused when I heard the sentence about* _____. Have the author reread the piece without the unfocused sentence. If there are many unfocused sentences, make a note to conference individually with the student during the next writing workshop.

Chart

**Primary Lesson
for
*The Big Block of Chocolate***

The Circus

Yesterday I went to the circus. There were lions, tigers, horses, and clowns with big, red feet in the three rings. My favorite color is red. The lions were roaring loudly. My sister is loud. The tigers were jumping through hoops of fire. My grandpa has a fireplace. The clowns were riding little, bitty tricycles and throwing confetti. There was so much happening at one time it was hard to see it all. I like to play baseball after school because it is a fun thing to do in my neighborhood. If you like to watch lots of action, the circus is a place that you should go!

The Big Block of Chocolate

by Janet Slater Redhead

Intermediate Lesson

Materials:

The Big Block of Chocolate, chart paper, markers, students' notebooks and writing folders

Mini-lesson:

focus on a topic

Mini-lesson

A. Build background.

Introduce the concept of focus by discussing with students times when you used an overhead projector and had to adjust the knob which made the print clear, or times when they have used a camera or binoculars and had to make adjustments so the subject would be clearly seen in the lens. Explain that in all three examples it was important to *focus* on the subject to see or understand it clearly. Teachers may wish to demonstrate with an overhead projector or a pair of binoculars.

Explain to students that a writer must apply the same effort in writing to focus on a topic. If the focus isn't clear, the reader will be confused and will not understand the purpose and meaning of the message. If the focus is clear, the reader can understand it easily.

Remind students that readers make predictions about what the writing is about based on the title of a book, short story, or newspaper article. As the writing unfolds, the title makes more sense. But if the writing does not relate to the title, we are left wondering why the author chose a title that didn't match the focus of the writing.

In the same manner, if you read an expository book about ocean life you expect that the content of the book will only be about ocean life. You should not read anything about African land mammals, how the space shuttle was built, or how to play baseball because these topics are not the focus of the book about ocean life.

You may wish to use a narrative example as well. If you are reading the story of Cinderella, you would not expect the author to add in something about Snow White or playing football because these things have nothing to do with Cinderella's story.

Conclude by stating that the topic of a piece of writing should match the contents of the writing, and all of the contents should be focused on the topic.

B. Introduce book and author.

Read the title aloud. Invite students to make predictions about the focus of the book.

Tell students that as you read the book aloud, they should jot down anything that does not match the focus of the book.

C. Read book aloud.

D. Discuss the following.

Ask students what they determined to be the focus of the book.

Ask students to share anything they heard which did not match the focus.

Review what happened to the block of chocolate. (Four different characters had the chocolate but decided to save it for a later time. Finally, when the chocolate melted, the ants did not hesitate to eat it.) Note that every event had to do with the same block of chocolate.

Discuss a few examples of events that would have been off-topic, such as the following questions.

What if Miss Jenny had bought popcorn?

What if Miss Jenny's dog found the apples on the shelf and took one of those instead?

What if the cat ate the chocolate and became very sick?

Student responses should indicate that none of the above would have been appropriate for the focus of the book.

Conclude by stating that a strong focus in expository or narrative literature allows the reader to understand and enjoy the writing fully. If writing is not focused, the reader will be confused and bored.

Quiet Writing/Conferencing

Ask students to think about some of their favorite foods and then to pick one they would like to write about. Remind students that they are composing expository pieces. In these expository pieces, students may choose to describe their favorite foods or explain how to prepare them. For an example, see the chart which follows the Sharing portion of the lesson.

Students should make jot lists of details that describe their favorite foods. Then students will use the details in complete sentences to form focused paragraphs that describe their favorite foods. If they begin to write about times when they enjoyed their favorite foods, the writing becomes narrative and is off-topic.

Begin using the students' pieces to apply the skills in these lessons. For example, have the students choose pieces already begun or allow them to revisit finished pieces. Ask them to reread the pieces looking at the focus. Tell students to determine whether the focus is clear or needs revision.

Sharing

Before each student shares a piece, first ask which food was chosen as the topic. Ask the student to share the personal jot list of details so that the other students can listen for the focused connection between the details and the topic. Then have the student share the paragraph description. After the student shares, model how to ask questions and how to offer valuable comments. Invite the class to do the same.

Students should continue to store their writing in their writing folders. By now they should have a small collection which they can revisit during future writing workshops.

Chart

Intermediate Lesson
for
The Big Block of Chocolate

Favorite foods: pizza
                      Nachos
                      fettucini alfredo
                      chocolate covered pretzels
                      M & Ms

Topic: Nachos
            Doritos, cool ranch
            cheddar, colby, or monterey jack cheese
            crunchy chips
            warm, melted cheese
            sliced black olives
            sour cream
            guacamole, creamy or chunky
            no jalapeño peppers!
            refried beans
            layers

Nachos are one of my favorite foods. When I make them at home I use Cool Ranch Doritos for the chips. I spread a thick layer of the chips on a plate. Then I spoon some refried beans over the chips. Next, I sprinkle some kind of cheese, such as cheddar, colby, or monterey jack cheese in a thick layer. Over the cheese, I spread sour cream and guacamole. Then I sprinkle some sliced or chopped black olives. The Nachos go in the microwave for two minutes, and I'm ready to dig in! When I order these in a restaurant, they are usually made the same way, but I ask the server to hold the jalapeños. Those peppers are way too hot for me!

The Important Book

by Margaret Wise Brown

Primary Lesson

Materials:

The Important Book, artificial flower, interviewing worksheets for each student, transparency or large chart of the interview worksheet, marker, pencils, notebook, writing folders or notebooks, paper

Mini-lesson:

focus

Mini-lesson

A. Build background.

Hold up an artificial flower up so all students can see it clearly. Ask students to focus on the flower and only the flower. What do they see? What would be important to say about a flower? Responses will include the color, the size, the shape, the name.

Next, ask why their responses didn't include the color of the teacher's hair or what the teacher was wearing. The answer is because they were instructed to focus only on the flower. The hair color or the clothes of the teacher has nothing to do with the flower.

Explain that by sharing only the details about the flower they were practicing a skill good writers use, called focus. When an author writes details only about the topic, the reader doesn't get confused about what the topic of the piece is intended to be. The author is sharing writing which has a clear focus.

B. Introduce the book and author.

Show the cover of the book and point out the word *important.*

Explain that the book shares important details about many different objects. Just as with the flower, the author focuses on one item and writes words about that item only.

Tell students that each page is almost like a riddle. Ask them to listen for the words that describe each item and notice how they are so clear and focused that it is easy to know what the author is writing about.

C. Read the book aloud.

Read the first page of the book, leaving out the noun. Example: *The important thing about a _____ is that you eat with it. It's like a little shovel. You hold it in your hand. You can put it in your mouth. It isn't flat. It's hollow and it spoons things up. But the important thing about a _____ is that you eat with it.*

Ask students to guess what the author is referring to. Reread the page, inserting the noun to cross-check their guesses.

Continue this pattern of reading throughout the book. To vary it, you can give students the name of the item and ask them to brainstorm important details focused on that item. Then read

Margaret Wise Brown's description to see if she included some of the same details.

D. Check for focus.

Show the page of the book that describes the spoon. Ask students why the author didn't write that a knife is sharp and you can cut meat with it. (The page isn't about a knife, it is about a spoon.)

Show the picture of the rain. Ask why the author didn't write that the sun is round and makes your eyes squint when you look at it. (The page isn't about the sun, it is about the rain.) The author did not lose her focus.

E. Model the skill.

Have each student find a partner and sit facing each other. Explain that they are going to focus on their partners and discover the important things about them.

Introduce the worksheet found behind the Sharing section of this lesson. It can be made into a transparency or written on a large sheet of chart paper.

The teacher should choose a partner and model how to fill out the interview sheet.

Model questions like:
What do you like to eat?
What is your favorite game?
What are the most important things that make you, you?

Choose two to three of the responses from above and record them on the worksheet in front of the class. Developing writers might notice that Margaret Wise Brown began and ended each page with the same sentence. They should be encouraged to do the same.

Quiet Writing/Conferencing

Students will complete the interview sheets with their partners. Remind them to stay focused only on their partner.

During quiet writing, students can continue their pieces about their friends or choose new topics. Encourage them to check their pieces often for focus by asking friends to listen to their pieces. If the friends can tell the authors in one sentence or less what the pieces are about, the writing probably is focused.

Sharing

Have students share their worksheets and have the audience guess who they are describing. Ask the audience why they guessed who they did. The interview sheets then could be bound to make a class book. Reinforce the concept that focus makes writing much clearer.

The important thing about

is _____

_____

_____

_____

_____

_____

but the important thing about

is _____

_____

_____

_____

The Important Book

by Margaret Wise Brown

Intermediate Lesson

Materials:

The Important Book, chart paper, markers, students' notebooks and writing folders

Mini-lesson:

focus on a topic

Mini-lesson

A. Build background.

Ask students to think of one thing that is important to them and how they might describe it. Share a few responses.

Now ask students to think of two or three things that are important and how they might describe all of these at the same time.

Conclude with students that the second task is more difficult because the focus is on more than one topic.

Tell students that writers need to focus their writing on one specific topic so that the reader may understand the message.

B. Introduce book and author.

Tell students that the author has focused the entire book on the title. They will need to listen and determine how she was able to do this.

Tell students that Margaret Wise Brown will also show them how to focus their writing on one specific item at a time.

C. Read book aloud.

D. Discuss the following.

Ask students to describe how the title of the book matched its contents. Students should recognize that each page began with the words *The important thing about...* They should also note that the last sentence on each page began with the same phrase.

Ask students to describe what they noticed about each page in the book. Students should recognize that each page was focused only on the item introduced in the first sentence on that page.

Tell students that you are going to reread a few pages. They are to listen for anything not focused on the specific topic. After each example, pause and share the response. Students should note that none of the information is off-topic.

Now read another page to the students, but insert a sentence that does not belong on the page. For example, on the page about the spoon, insert a sentence about a fork. On the page about snow, insert a sentence about ice cubes. Students should be able to identify the off-topic sentence in each example.

Discuss with students why it is so important to stay focused in our writing. Guide them to see that off-focus and off-topic information can be confusing for the reader.

Quiet Writing/Conferencing

Model with the students how to write a focused paragraph on one topic. Share examples from the chart that follows the Sharing portion of the lesson. Students then will choose to write about things that are important to them. Encourage students to try the pattern Margaret Wise Brown modeled in her book and in the examples on the chart. Remind students that this is an expository piece of writing.

Students will need to see the importance of focus in narrative writing as well. On another day have them choose narrative pieces from their folders and check the focus of the pieces.

Sharing

In preparing students for sharing, tell them that they are going to read their pieces as riddles. When it is their turn to share, ask them to leave out the name of the topic every time it appears in the writing. Model how to do this with one of the examples on the chart.

> *The important thing about a _____ is that it holds all my school supplies.*

When each student has shared a paragraph, the others should have heard enough focused details to determine the topic of the riddle. As you proceed with sharing, ask students to comment on which details had the strongest focus.

As the students share narrative pieces of writing, ask the class to listen carefully for the focus. During sharing time, take the opportunity to note how each writer focused on one topic only and did not try to bring in pieces of information that were off focus.

Chart

Intermediate Lesson
for
The Important Book

The important thing about a *desk* is that it holds all my school supplies. It waits for me every morning. Sometimes other people use it during the day, but no one uses it at night. Every year I get a new one, and the teacher makes sure it is the right size for me. It has four legs and a flat top. I do my writing and math on it. I use it to color and design my artwork, and I may tap on it during music. But the important thing about a *desk* is that it holds all my school supplies.

The important thing about my *shoelaces* is that they are soft and bendable and come in pairs. They are usually white, but can be other colors or designs. They go in and out of holes to hold things together and have a hard tip at each end. I use two fingers to put them together, but sometimes they come undone. If they come undone, I may trip. But the important thing about my *shoelaces* is that they are soft and bendable and come in pairs.

Little Cloud

by Eric Carle

Primary Lesson

Materials:

Little Cloud, one 4" x 6" piece of plain, white construction paper for every student, one 18" x 24" piece of white construction paper, large piece of chart paper, marker, pencils, paper, writing folders, or notebooks

Mini-lesson:

focus on a topic

Mini-lesson

A. Build background.

Go outside and look at the clouds, or look at the clouds through a window. Have students return to their seats, close their eyes, and picture the cloud in their heads. Ask them to focus their minds on the cloud.

Then have them open their eyes and share the words that popped into their heads as they thought about the cloud.

Ask for words that would describe what they saw. As the students share, write the words or phrases on a large piece of chart paper. After all students have shared, reread the chart.

Make note that all the words relate to a cloud. The chart is focused on the topic of clouds. Explain that means there are only words or phrases on the chart that refer to clouds.

B. Introduce the book and the author.

Show the cover of the book, and point out the picture of the cloud. Tell the students that the author, Eric Carle, has written an entire book about a cloud. To write this book, he probably closed his eyes and focused on one little cloud just as they had done.

Ask students to listen as the story is read to hear if Eric Carle stayed focused on his topic, a little cloud.

C. Read the book aloud.

D. Discuss the following.

Ask two or three students to share, in one sentence, what the topic of the book was. They should answer that the book is about a little cloud, or the book is about how a little cloud changes.

Ask the class why they answered as they did. Note that all the sentences in the book were about the little cloud and how it changed into a sheep, airplane, shark, etc.

Ask why the author didn't put anything in his story about a caterpillar turning into a butterfly. The story wasn't about a caterpillar; it was about a little cloud. Some students might mention however, that Eric Carle has another book that is focused on a caterpillar called *The Very Hungry Caterpillar*.

E. Model the skill.

Give each child a white piece of construction paper. Have the students tear their papers into shapes that resemble clouds. Do the same with a large sheet of construction paper.

Hang the large cloud beside the chart composed during Building Background. Tell the class they are going to write their own little cloud pieces.

Reread the chart with the words describing attributes of a cloud generated earlier. Then point out the large cloud shape made by the teacher. Write *My Cloud* at the top of the shape. Instruct students to do the same. Use guided writing with kindergarten students, isolating the sounds, then writing the letters to spell *My Cloud*.

Next, have students look for words on the chart that would help readers see the same cloud they saw. Model for the students how to use words on the previous chart to generate a focused sentence about a cloud. For example, a phrase on the chart might read *looks like cotton*.

On the cloud write *My cloud looks just like cotton*. Ask why it wouldn't make sense to write *Cotton candy looks just like cotton*. The answer is because the topic is *My Cloud*, not *My Cotton Candy*.

Continue modeling under the first sentence using examples like *soft* and *big*. Write *It looks soft like a pillow. It takes up the sky, it is so big.*

Quiet Writing/Conferencing

Reread what has been written so far on the large cloud. Ask students if all the sentences are focused on the topic. Finally, have them use the chart to write sentences on their own clouds.

Early emergent writers may write only three or four words. Encourage them to use phonetic spelling to write their words and not to copy them from the chart. Early writers may write three or four sentences. The aim is to have students concentrate on the topic of a cloud, write sentences that are focused on the subject of a cloud, and not to stray from that topic.

As students continue their quiet, independent writing, allow them to add on to their cloud pieces, look back at previous pieces in their writing folders for focus, or begin new pieces of writing. Remind them to include only words or sentences that are about the topic they choose.

Sharing

Have three to four students share their cloud pieces. Have the audience signal thumbs-up if the piece had words or sentences focused on a cloud. Have them hold their thumb sideways if there were one or two sentences that seemed off-focus. Have them point thumbs-down if the piece was about something else besides clouds. Have students who hold a thumb sideways or down share with the author why they thought some sentences were off-focus. Have students who signal a thumbs-up explain why they thought the writing was focused.

Little Cloud

by Eric Carle

Intermediate Lesson

Materials:

Little Cloud, chart paper, markers, students' notebooks and writing folders

Mini-lesson:

focus on a topic

Mini-lesson

A. Build background.

Discuss with students things they notice about clouds when they see them. Record their responses on chart paper in jot list form. Encourage students to think about size, shape, color, and movement.

When the list has several characteristics noted, tell students to reread the list to themselves, but cover up the topic. Ask them if they would be able to tell that this entire list of words all had to do with the same topic and how they would know. See sample chart which follows the Sharing portion.

Explain to the students that by focusing on the sole topic of clouds, they have just practiced an important thinking skill which all writers must use.

B. Introduce book and author.

Tell students that Eric Carle does the same thing they have done by staying focused on one topic.

Read and discuss the title of the book. Ask students what they think *Little Cloud* is and what it is about.

Tell students that as you read the book aloud, they should determine which of their notes about clouds appears in Eric Carle's book.

C. Read book aloud.

D. Discuss the following.

Ask students how the title matched the contents of the book.

Compare Eric Carle's description of Little Cloud to the list of notes generated by the class. Discuss how both are focused only on one topic.

Quiet Writing/Conferencing

Ask students to choose an object in nature such as a tree, the wind, the beach, or a squirrel to compose expository pieces of writing. Encourage them to think about size, shape, color, movement, or any other characteristics of their topic. Brainstorm a list of details which are focused on the topic. Then use the details in complete sentences to compose a focused paragraph.

For another lesson on focus, have the students choose narrative pieces from their folders to check for focus. They will work on evaluating how well the pieces are focused on their respective topics. Ask them to make any necessary revisions.

Sharing

As students share, make note of the types of details used to focus on their topics. This will help you determine valuable questions to model for the class. For example, if a student's piece is entirely focused on what a tree looks like, ask if the focus was meant to be just on what the tree looks like, or was it meant to be an entire description of the tree. If the latter is the answer, nudge the writer into thinking about how the tree smells, or which animals live in it, or how it sounds when the wind sways the branches. You also should make note of strong, focused details, and model how to comment on them.

Please note that this lesson and the information in the Sharing portion create a transition to the next section of lessons on elaboration.

Chart

Intermediate Lesson
for
Little Cloud

Topic: Clouds

white

gray

fluffy

cotton balls

pink sunset streaks

swirls

wisps

silent

rushing

quietly sailing

filled with rain

funnels

towers

black

angry

willowy

ribbons

marshmallows

CHAPTER THREE

Elaboration

This section of mini-lessons focuses on developing elaboration skills.

Elaboration is defined as the act of developing detail carefully and thoroughly. Details are describing words or phrases. Student writers in kindergarten through fifth grades may learn how to introduce several kinds of details to their writing. Some categories are alliteration, simile, metaphor, and onomatopoeia. Authors may use a combination of these devices to create rich, descriptive language, such as is found in *Owl Moon*. Another way to develop descriptive language is simply to fine and learn new words, such as in *Alexander and the Terrible, Horrible, No Good, Very Bad Day*. The goal of these lessons is to expose students to elaboration skills that give their writing detailed meaning.

Familiarize yourself with the following terms, and use the information to begin planning for these lessons. It is likely that examples of these tools for elaboration appear in students' reading materials. Look for evidence of them, and encourage students to do the same. This will help them see the value of elaboration in expository and narrative writing, as well as fiction and non-fiction.

Alliteration is a series of words with the same beginning sound. Popular examples are found in tongue-twisters, such as *Sally sells seashells by the seashore*. Alliteration captures the reader's attention. The reader dwells a little longer on those words because of the rhythm of their sound.

Kindergarten students should be working to identify beginning sounds and learn the sounds that accompany letters. You should expect kindergarten students to identify two words that have the same beginning sound.

By the time students are in second grade they should be able to compose two or more words in sequence with the same beginning sound that make sense. Fourth-grade students should be able to compose complete sentences with an example of alliteration.

Throughout all the grade levels, it is important to emphasize to students that the alliteration example needs to carry meaning. A random string of words with the same initial sound does not constitute a meaningful example of alliteration.

Similes are a comparison of one item to another using the word *like* or *as* to complete the comparison. Examples are *My pillow is as soft as a feather*, or *My pillow is soft like a feather*. Depending on the language development of the students, the comparison will reflect a level of awareness which grows from experience. A first grader may write, *I was as happy as a clown*, while a fourth grader may write, *I was as sleepy as a bear hibernating in his cave*. Writers use similes to help the reader make a connection between an idea the reader has experience with and the message in the writing.

Metaphor is also a comparison of one item to another, but it does not include *like* or *as* to complete the comparison. To eliminate confusion, introduce the concept of metaphor after students understand simile. An example of metaphor is *Her smile was a bright light to me*. As with similes, this type of elaboration requires experience and vocabulary. A first grader may write, *The sun was a yellow ball*, where a fifth grader may write, *The smell of the daisy was a sweet perfume in the air*.

Onomatopoeia is a word that stands for a sound. They are sound words, but not words that describe sounds. There is a difference, and it may take practice for students to observe that difference. An example of a word which describes sound would be found in a sentence such as, *That old door squeaks when it opens*. Revising this with onomatopoeia would result in this sentence: *As I opened the door I heard, 'Squeeeak!* or, *As I opened the door, an eerie squeak filled the silence*.

Students of all grade levels have fun with this because they become storytellers as they sound out the sound words. Some easy topics to generate the use of onomatopoeia are holidays, animals, and stormy days.

After exploring and enjoying these lessons, you may guide students to conclude that an essential part of elaboration is a writer's word choice. It is important and appropriate to help young writers learn how to make good word choices for their pieces. The next lesson in this section is about specific word choice.

In addition to the skills explained above, two lessons in this section fit the more general category of descriptive language. Elaboration techniques include more than patterns for words. The books cited in this section contain highly effective strings of words and patterns that create enjoyable text. They may have a simile or two, but the overall language is descriptive in a non-patterned way.

The lessons in this section are meant to be used to introduce, or reinforce, the elaboration skills explained above. Below-average students will need many more experiences with these skills to be able to choose when and where to use them. Average students will be able to use these skills now and then. Above-average students will apply these skills almost immediately, having fun all the while. Teachers need to decide when it is appropriate to introduce the terms and when to expect students to use the terms as part of their writer's vocabulary.

Although the terms alliteration, onomatopoeia, simile, and metaphor have to do with the technique of describing a topic, many of the words that students will choose to use are adjectives. You may wish to use the adjective lesson in the Conventions section as the beginning point for understanding the function of this part of speech. Then have fun exploring the many ways of using adjectives in writing.

Regardless of the grade level, remember to expose students to many kinds of elaboration techniques. The more they hear and see how language may be used, the more background is collected in the writer's mind. When the writer is ready, these skills will appear on paper.

Other books that may be used to model elaboration skills:

> *In the Small, Small Pond* by Denise Fleming
> *Grandma According to Me* by Karen Magnuson Bell

A Walk in the Rainforest

by Kristin Joy Pratt

Primary Lesson

Materials:

A Walk in the Rainforest, writing folder or notebook, paper, pencils, chart paper, colored marker, teacher prepared chart of descriptions using alliteration found behind the sharing section

Mini-lesson:

alliteration

Mini-lesson

A. Build background.

Ask students to repeat after you, *She sells seashells down by the seashore.* Ask what sounds were repeated.

Ask students to repeat after you, *How much wood could a woodchuck chuck if a woodchuck could chuck wood?* Ask what sounds were repeated.

Explain that both sentences contain examples of alliteration. Alliteration means choosing words that begin with the same sound and putting these together into a sentence that makes sense. It's fun for authors to write and fun for people to hear and read.

B. Introduce the book and the author.

Explain the book is about all the unusual animals who make their homes in the rainforest. It is full of information about these animals. It is a non-fiction book.

Explain the author, Kristin Pratt, writes about these animals by using alliteration on every page to describe them.

Ask students to listen closely for words that begin with the same sound in every sentence of the book.

C. Read the book aloud.

As you read, stop now and then and ask students to identify the repeated sound. For example, on page three read, *a beautiful Bromeliad with a bright red center.* Ask what sound was repeated more than once. Students should answer that the *b* sound was used three times.

D. Show the chart.

Before the lesson, prepare Chart One found following the Sharing section of this lesson. You also can prepare a master so each student could have a personal chart to work with.

Instruct students to listen for alliteration as each sentence is read aloud. Underline the matching beginning sounds with a colored marker. Repeat only the words that are underlined.

Identify the sound once more. Teachers of emergent writers may wish to stop here and move into quiet writing. Students would be ready to begin Section E on the following day.

E. Model the skill.

On a clean sheet of chart paper, write the word *bear*. Have students brainstorm words that would describe a bear and begin with a *b*. Examples might include *big, brown, busy, bad,* or *bully*. If students are unable to volunteer their own words, you should add them to the chart paper.

Next, model how to take the words on the chart and compose them into a sentence. Using the bear example, the sentence would read, *The big, brown bear was bad.* Repeat the example using the word *snake*. Students should generate words beginning with an *s* that describe a snake. Examples might include *slippery, slimy, silly, slithering,* or *super*.

Again, model how to use these words to generate a sentence about a snake. An example might be *A snake can be slippery, slimy, and slithering.* Continue this activity using any animal or object. Emergent writers will benefit from watching the teacher write using the procedure above. Developing writers can write their own sentences independently or in small groups after the teacher models the previous examples. Allow developing writers five minutes to compose. Then ask students to share their sentences aloud.

Quiet Writing/Conferencing

Move students into quiet individual writing. Emergent writers may want to illustrate the sentences generated from the modeling section. Then encourage them to try their own sentences using alliteration under the illustration. These sentences with the illustrations could be bound together to make a class book.

While conferencing with developing writers, point out opportunities for alliteration to describe the person, place, or object in their piece of writing.

Consider using the activities described above to write in a content area. Using alliteration to share scientific facts or math problems provides a different sort of practice. For example, *The plant grows giant green roots into the ground,* or *Adding one active antelope and one angry ape equals two animals.* These are examples of expository writing.

Using alliteration to describe the setting or the character provides practice for narrative writing as well. You can use these activities for another writing workshop that models alliteration.

Sharing

Invite all students who tried alliteration in their writing to share that particular section of their piece of writing. Encourage all students to use alliteration to describe attributes of a person, animal, or object, in their writing during the next week.

Chart

**Primary Lesson
for
*A Walk in the Rainforest***

A feathery fern on the forest floor.

A gentle giant gorilla grinning in the green growth.

A jumbo jaguar just about ready to jump.

A slow sloth suspended in a tree.

Wonderfully wet water washing over the rocks.

A Walk in the Rainforest

by Kristin Joy Pratt

Intermediate Lesson

Materials:

A Walk in the Rainforest, two or three tongue-twisters, chart paper, markers, dictionaries, students' notebooks and writing folders

Mini-lesson:

alliteration

Mini-lesson

A. Build background.

Ask students if they have ever heard of tongue-twisters. Share a few tongue-twisters.

Ask students what they notice about tongue-twisters that makes them different from other types of writing they have practiced.

Discuss the fact that tongue-twisters not only have a string of words beginning with the same sound, but the string of words also has meaning. Therefore, a tongue-twister cannot be just a series of words beginning with the same sound.

Explain to students that tongue-twisters are an example of writing known as alliteration. One way to use alliteration is with tongue twisters, but it may be used effectively in narrative and expository writing as well.

B. Introduce book and author.

Share with students the information about the author on the back cover.

Tell students that Kristin Joy Pratt's book has many examples of alliteration. They should listen carefully, and jot down one or two favorite examples of alliteration as you read the book.

C. Read book aloud.

D. Discuss the following.

Ask students what they noticed about the author's use of alliteration. Guide them to conclude that the book is a non-fiction alphabet book of living things found in the rainforest.

Invite students to share some of their favorite examples of alliteration in the book. Record their responses on chart paper. See sample chart which follows the Sharing portion.

After writing several examples, go back and highlight the words that form the alliteration in each example. Some sentences have more than one example of alliteration.

Emphasize that these examples of alliteration have a meaning-ful message. They are not just a string of words that begin with the same sound.

E. Model writing an alliteration sentence. See example on chart.

Choose a letter and think of a noun, such as an animal that begins with that letter, and write it.

Think of an adjective to describe the noun and write it in front of the first word.

Think about and write a verb to describe the action of the noun.

Think about and write a preposition, such as *around, over, between*, etc.

Choose another adjective and another noun. Make sure to put in a capital letter and period.

Quiet Writing/Conferencing

Ask students to write two to three sentences that include alliteration. They may wish to use their initials or other favorite letters for the sounds to develop the alliteration. Remind students that the sequence of words needs to be meaningful.

Tell students to use a dictionary for help with finding words to complete their sentences.

Point out that alliterative examples are fun to write and that they may be used in both narrative and expository writing. Examples of narrative alliteration, such as tongue-twisters, usually involve a character and something the character does. Expository examples of alliteration could be a description of an animal, the weather, or the mountains. Encourage students to revisit pieces of writing in their folders and find appropriate places to incorporate meaningful alliteration.

Sharing

As students share their examples of alliteration encourage the class to comment on the word choice used in the pieces of writing. Once students understand how to apply this skill, teachers may wish to create a class alliteration alphabet. List the letters of the alphabet down the left side of pieces of chart paper. Invite the students to sign up for a letter to write about. For more difficult letters, such as Q, X, and Z, students may wish to work with a partner to compose the alliterative example.

Chart

Intermediate Lesson
for
A Walk in the Rainforest

Examples of alliteration from book

   an intriguing Iguana basking on a branch (2 examples)
   a jumbo Jaguar just about ready to jump (1 example)
   a gentle giant Gorilla grinning in the green growth (2 examples)
   a feathery Fern on the forest floor (1 example)
   wonderfully wet Water washing over the rocks (1 example)
   a vibrant Vanilla Orchid with very flavorful fruit (2 examples)

Composing a sentence with alliteration

   a letter: s
   a noun: skunk
   an adjective: striped
   a verb: scampers
   a preposition: between
   another adjective and noun: silvery stones

   Sentence: A striped skunk scampers between silvery stones.

Quick As a Cricket

by Audrey Wood

Primary Lesson

Materials:

Quick As a Cricket, bag containing a star, stuffed cat, sugar in a plastic, closeable bag, fake grass, ribbon, large sheet of chart paper, notes that stick to paper, marker, pencils, writing folders or notebooks, paper.

Mini-lesson:

similes

Mini-lesson

A. Build background.

Write the word *simile* on chart paper. Ask for suggestions about what the word might mean. Accept all responses. Point to the word and explain that a simile is a way writers compare one thing to another using the word *as* or *like*.

Explain that writers do this to allow the reader to get a clearer picture in their heads of the story being told. Using similes is a way of describing a setting, person, animal, or feeling in a special way that is more interesting to the reader.

B. Introduce the book and the author.

Point out the cricket and the boy on the cover. Ask if the class agrees that a cricket is quick. Ask for suggestions of other quick things.

Explain that the boy in the story compares himself to a cricket because he thinks he is quick. Ask students to listen as the story is read for all the other comparisons the boy uses to describe himself.

C. Read the story aloud.

D. Discuss the following.

Ask a volunteer to name what the author had the boy continually compare himself to. (The answer is *animals*.) Ask if the author used the words *like* or *as*.

Reread a few pages and let the students fill in the animal. For example, *I'm as slow as a _____*. The class would read aloud, *snail*.

E. Model the skill.

Explain that an author can use many things for comparisons when writing a simile. Show the bag with the star, stuffed cat, sugar, etc. Tell the class they are going to write some similes using the items in the bag.

Pull out the star. Ask for characteristics of a star. (Examples: pointed, shiny, big, blue. Write these characteristics on the large sheet of chart paper. Choose one of these and model on the same piece of chart paper how to write a simile. Example: *It was as pointed as a star.*)

Next, tell the class it is their turn. Pass out stick-on notes to each student, and have them write their own similes in the format, *It was as _____ as a star*. Have students place their completed notes on the piece of chart paper.

Read each note aloud. Continue this process with every item in the bag.

F. **Guide students into writing more specific similes with this activity.**

Think of something that would be as pointed as a star. Write these suggestions on another piece of chart paper. (Examples: *nose, pencil, snowflake*.) Choose one of the student examples and model how to write a different simile. (Example: *His nose was as pointed as a star*.)

Pass out new sticky notes, and have students write new similes, replacing the word *it*. Place them on the chart. Read these aloud. Continue this process for every item in the bag.

G. **To allow students to practice writing similes using like, follow parts E and F on a different day. Substitute the word like for as to write new similes.**

Quiet Writing/Conferencing

Tell students that they have now written many similes using the word *as* to help with descriptions. As students move into independent quiet writing, encourage them to try similes in their own writing. Allow them to choose their own topics to experiment with similes, or suggest using similes during quiet writing to describe themselves as the boy did in the book.

Sharing

Invite students to share their similes.

Have them read their descriptions with and without the simile. For example: *The moon is round. The moon is as round as a ball.* Model how to recognize comparison with a simile by saying, *I noticed that you compared _____ to a_____*. An example would be *I noticed that you compared the moon to a round ball.*

Quick as a Cricket

by Audrey Wood

Intermediate Lesson

Materials:

Quick as a Cricket, chart paper, markers, students' notebooks, and writing folders

Mini-lesson:

similes

Mini-lesson

A. Build background.

Ask students if they have ever thought about comparing themselves to animals. Perhaps they thought about how they are like fish when they are swimming, or a cheetah when they are running, or a monkey when they climb trees. Share a few responses.

B. Introduce book and author.

Tell students that you have a special book that is all about comparing a person to many different animals.

Ask students to look for a word pattern in Audrey Wood's book as you read.

C. Read book aloud.

D. Discuss the following.

Ask students how the title of the book matched its contents. Ask students if they noticed a pattern on each page. They should respond that each page uses the word *as* to make a comparison.

Go back and reread a few pages, noting that each comparison connects the person to the animal by using the word *as*, an adjective, and the word *as* again. Explain that this form of comparison is known as *simile*. See chart which follows the Sharing portion.

Reread a few more pages, but leave out the last two words. Invite students to respond with their own words to finish the simile. (Example: *I'm as loud as...*) Record their responses on chart paper.

Explain to students that similes may also use the word *like* to make a comparison.

Rewrite a few pages from the book as examples of similes using *like*.

Explain to students that similes may be used in expository or narrative writing to illustrate effective comparisons. Think about the topics the class is studying in science or social studies. Point out that similes may be used in non-fiction text to support the description of a topic such as a land form, the weather, or the rainforest. Think about using similes in narrative writing as an elaboration tool for building character descriptions.

Conclude by restating the definition of simile.

Quiet Writing/Conferencing

Ask students to make a jot list of ten words that describe themselves. Then have them think of an animal, person, or object which is similar to them. Use the words *as* or *like* to compose ten similes about themselves.

Encourage students to try applying similes in other pieces of expository and narrative writing.

Sharing

As students share their pieces, have the class ask appropriate questions and offer comments about the writing. Record several student samples of similes on chart paper, and post in the classroom as a resource.

Chart

Intermediate Lesson
for
Quick as a Cricket

Simile = a comparison of two things using *as* or *like*

<u>Examples using *as*</u>

I'm as quick as _____ .

I'm as weak as _____ .

I'm as cold as _____ .

I'm as loud as _____ .

I'm as gentle as _____ .

<u>Examples using *like*</u>

I'm slow like _____ .

I'm strong like _____ .

I'm hot like _____ .

I'm quiet like _____ .

I'm tough like _____ .

Say Something

by Mary Stolz

Primary Lesson

Materials:

Say Something, chart paper, marker for teacher and for eight small groups, pencils, American flag, crayon, eight sheets of white construction paper, writing folders or notebooks, paper

Mini-lesson:

metaphors

Mini-lesson

A. Build background.

Tell students that writers often compare one thing to another when they are describing a person, place, or thing in their writing. They do this to help the reader get a crystal-clear picture in their mind of that person, place, or thing.

Explain that one way writers paint these crystal-clear pictures is with metaphors. Metaphors are a group of words that compare two things having something in common by using the words *is, are,* or *am.*

B. Introduce the book and the author.

Ask the class to listen for any metaphors — comparisons between two items.

C. Read the book aloud.

Read just the first page and stop. Ask for a volunteer who heard the metaphor. Ask what the cave was compared to. Ask why the author would say that a cave is a deep darkness.

Read the second page. Ask a volunteer to say what the grass was compared to. Ask why the author would compare grass to a green living room.

Read the third page. Ask for a volunteer who heard the metaphor to explain why the author would compare a brook to a watery hallway.

Next, read the sentence that says, *Say something about a tadpole.* Ask students to brainstorm what the author might compare to a tadpole. Read the next page to see if any of their predictions were correct.

The next page contains no metaphors. Point that out to the students if they do not notice. Continue reading the book, stopping on each page to discuss the comparisons.

D. Model the skill.

Show the class a pencil. Ask the class to say something about a pencil using a metaphor. Write all suggestions on the top half of a large sheet of chart paper.

Choose one or two of the students' suggestions and write a metaphor about a pencil using the students' suggestions. An example might be, *The pencil is a long, yellow stick.*

Show the students a globe. Ask the class to say something about a globe. Write all suggestions on the bottom half of the chart paper.

Choose one or two of the student suggestions and write a metaphor about a globe. An example might be *A globe is a green and blue ball.*

Divide students into groups of four.

Ask each group to think about the sun and record on their papers what could be said about the sun. After five minutes, have each group use their lists to compose a metaphor about the sun. Have each group share their metaphor.

Quiet Writing/Conferencing

Tell students, as they move into independent writing, to try composing a metaphor when describing a person, animal, or object. Metaphors help readers have a better understanding of what is being described.

Metaphors lend themselves well to expository. For example, in a piece about animal facts, a student may compose, *A crab is a crawling shell.*

They are also helpful in narrative when a student describes a character or a setting. Examples: *My grandma is a hugging teddy bear,* or *The beach is a hot tamale.*

Sharing

Have students share any metaphors they composed. Ask the author what the comparison was. Put examples of metaphors on a large sheet of chart paper to allow students to model them. Metaphors also could be collected, illustrated, and made into a class book.

Say Something

by Mary Stolz

Intermediate Lesson

Materials:

Say Something, chart paper, two different colored markers, students' notebooks and writing folders

Mini-lesson:

metaphors

Mini-lesson

A. Build background.

If students have learned to write similes, begin with a review of the definition of simile. This will help clarify the difference between similes and this lesson on metaphors. Tell students we often describe something by comparing one item or concept to another. It helps the person we are communicating with to have a better understanding of our message.

When writers paint pictures in the reader's mind they too may choose to use comparisons between two items.

Write the word *metaphor* on chart paper. Tell students that metaphors are another tool that writers use for elaboration.

B. Introduce book and author.

Discuss the title, and predict what the book may be about. Tell students to listen carefully to the language and try to figure out the meaning of metaphor.

C. Read book aloud.

D. Discuss the following.

Ask students what they noticed about the pattern of the book. Invite a few students to share their own responses to *Say something about...* and write them on the chart paper. See example which follows the Sharing portion.

Ask what is being compared in each of the responses. Underline or circle these words in one color.

Ask students if there are any particular words which may be part of a pattern. At this point they may identify *is* as a word used in each of the comparisons.

Explain that a metaphor is a comparison of two things without using *like* or *as* (as in a simile), but it does use *is*, *are*, or *am*. Write this definition next to *metaphor* at the top of the chart.

Using a second color marker, highlight *is, are,* or *am* in the student examples of metaphors.

Explain to students that metaphor is an elaboration technique that may be used in expository or narrative writing to make a comparison.

Demonstrate the use for this skill in expository and non-fiction writing by examining topics the class is studying in science, health, math, and social studies. Consider the following examples.

A thunderstorm is a bowling game in the sky.
A rainforest is a damp living room for tropical animals.
Division is thirty kids sitting in six rows of five.

In narrative writing, metaphor may easily be used to compare characters. Share examples where an evil character might be compared to the Big Bad Wolf or Charlotte from *Charlotte's Web* might be described as Wilbur's hero.

Quiet Writing/Conferencing

Ask students to think about several things they like and to make jot lists of them. Then they will need to think of something to compare to each item. Finally, ask them to connect the pairs by inserting *is*, *are*, or *am* and adding details. Students should edit their metaphors and choose favorites to share.

Have students apply this skill to other pieces of writing. They may choose to revise expository or narrative pieces from their writing folders. Encourage them to look for one or two places where a metaphor might improve the message in the writing.

Sharing

As students share their metaphors, have the class respond with appropriate questions and comments. You may wish to ask the writer if the metaphor would fit in a piece of expository writing, narrative writing, or both. You may also consider having the students copy their metaphors on chart paper to be posted in the classroom. These examples serve as valuable resources for future writing.

Chart

Intermediate Lesson
for
Say Something

Metaphor = a comparison of two things using *is* or *are* or *am*

Examples of student responses

The night: The night is the sun's giant shadow.

Snow: Snow is the ground's cold, white blanket.

The moon: The moon is the brother of the earth and a cousin of the other planets.

My piano: My piano is a white and black key chain.

Dance: Dance is a tap-a, twirl-a, jazzy split.

A soccer ball: A soccer ball is a marshmallow covered in chocolate diamonds.

A house: A house is a place to store your life.

A butterfly: A butterfly is a spirit of the wind.

An umbrella: An umbrella is a mushroom cap and an old woman's cane.

The moon: The moon is a glowing night light in the dark sky.

The Listening Walk

by Paul Showers

Primary Lesson

Materials:

The Listening Walk, word card with sounds printed on them, chart paper, markers, paper, writing folders or notebooks, pencils

Mini-lesson:

onomatopoeia

Mini-lesson

A. Build background.

Pass out five pre-written word cards with the following sounds.

card one:	*rat-a-tat-tat*
card two:	*bzzzzzzzzzz*
card three:	*zooooooooom*
card four:	*waaaaaaaah*
card five:	*sssssssssssss*

Ask each student to read the card aloud. Kindergarten students may need assistance. Have the class repeat the sounds on the cards.

Explain the words they have just read show onomatopoeia. Words that make a sound just like the real person, animal, or thing are special words authors use to make their writing better. When a writer uses onomatopoeia, the reader can actually hear what is happening in the story.

B. Introduce the book and the author.

Tell the class they are about to take a listening walk. Because the walk is just a pretend-walk for them, the author must use onomatopoeia to allow all who read the story to hear all the sounds he did. Ask them to listen for those sounds.

C. Read the book aloud, stopping occasionally to identify examples of onomatopoeia.

D. Model the skill.

Return to the five cards used at the beginning of the lessons. Tape them across the top of a large piece of chart paper. Take each card one at a time and have students brainstorm all the things that would make that sound. For example, card one reads, *rat-a-tat-tat.* Students might suggest a woodpecker, a hammer, a pencil, or fingers can make this sound.

Write each example underneath the word card. Second graders might work in cooperative groups and do the same thing with a group chart. After examples have been given for each card, move this chart aside but leave it in view of all students.

Quiet Writing/Conferencing

Use a large, new sheet of chart paper to model how to use onomatopoeia in a sentence. Begin the sentence with one of the brainstormed words. For example, write, *The woodpecker*, then add, *went rat-a-tat-tat on my chimney*. Have students read the sentence together. Continue writing sentences combining the sound words on the cards and the list of words brainstormed by the class. Again, second graders could independently try this activity in cooperative groups after teacher modeling.

Send students to independent, quiet writing. Encourage them to try onomatopoeia in new pieces of writing. You could also suggest choosing pieces from previous writing workshops and try adding onomatopoeia to one of the sentences found there. Have students think about the person, animal, or object they will be writing about during writing workshop. Then ask them to think about the sound it would make as they try putting them together.

Onomatopoeia can be used in narrative or expository writing.

Sharing

Invite students who have tried using onomatopoeia to share their pieces of writing. Have them tell the audience how they chose the sound words they used. Model how to respond to the writing with, *I noticed you used the sound _____ in your writing so that the audience could hear the _____*. The class may want to start a class sound-word dictionary to refer to when using onomatopoeia.

The Listening Walk

by Paul Showers

Intermediate Lesson

Materials:

The Listening Walk, chart paper, markers, students' notebooks and writing folders

Mini-lesson:

onomatopoeia

Mini-lesson

A. Build background.

Ask students if they ever spend quiet time just listening to everything around them. What kinds of sounds do they hear? Share some responses.

Ask students to describe some sounds they like to hear and some sounds that are not enjoyable.

Tell students you have a book to share about a girl who loves to listen to many kinds of sounds.

B. Introduce book and author.

Ask students what they think a *listening walk* might be. Share a few responses.

Tell students to listen for all the sounds on *The Listening Walk.*

C. Read book aloud.

D. Discuss the following.

Ask students how the title matches the content of the book.

Discuss several sounds the girl heard on the listening walk. Go back to the first sounds mentioned (Major's toenails and father's shoes). Ask students if they have ever noticed these sounds. What sound words would they use to describe these sounds? List responses on chart paper as in the sample found after the Sharing portion.

Explain to students that sound words are examples of onomatopoeia.

Explain the difference between words that describe sounds and sound words. (For example: *The creaky door opened slowly.* Or, *Creak! Creak! The door opened slowly.*

Finish reviewing the book's examples of onomatopoeia. Have students create their own sound words. Add these to the chart.

Tell students that in quiet writing it will be their turn to listen to the sounds of school.

Quiet Writing/Conferencing

Take students out in the hallway and have them sit on the floor. If time allows, you may wish to take a listening walk through the school or even outside, around the school property. Give them five minutes to listen to the sounds of school and jot them down on their paper. When students come back to the classroom, have them compose a description of the sounds of school. Remind students that this piece of writing is expository. Encourage them to use onomatopoeia in their description.

Have students look for ways to use onomatopoeia in other pieces of writing from their writing folder. Tell them that this skill can effectively be used in narrative writing when describing the events, objects, or characters' voices of a story.

Sharing

As students share their pieces, notice how many different sounds the class shares, as well as how many students heard the same sounds. Ask students to comment on effective examples of onomatopoeia. You may wish to have students copy these examples on a class chart to be posted in the room. This list serves as a resource for future writing needs. Students may add to this list when they come across examples of onomatopoeia in expository or narrative text.

Invite students to share other pieces of writing which they revised with onomatopoeia. Ask them to read the original sentence first, then the revised one. Discuss with the class the difference in meaning. Ask students, *What did the first sentence make you think of? How did the revised sentence make you feel?* Students should see that the effective use of onomatopoeia affects the reader's imagination and enjoyment of the writing.

Chart

Intermediate Lesson
for
The Listening Walk

(You can copy all or some of these examples.)

<u>Examples from book</u>   <u>Student examples</u>

twick, twick, twick, twick

dop, dup, dop, dup

z-z-z-z-z-zzzzzzooooooooooooooommmm

thhhhhhhhhhhhhhhhhhhh

whithhh whithhh whithhh whithhh

hmmmmmmmmmm

brack-a brack-a brack-a brack-a

whhrrrrrrrrrrrrrrr

eeeeeeeeeeeeeeeeee

trring trring

waaaa awaaaa awaaaa awaaaa

eeeeeeeyowwwooooooooooooooooo

bomp bomp bomp bomp

bik bok bik bok bik bok

bik bik bik bik bik bik

pfssssss

chrrooooooooooooffff

dak - dak - dak - dak - dak - dak - dak

chuff chuff chuff chuff

prrrooo prrrooo prrrooo prrrooo

gank gank wonk wonk gank gank

gaaaaank gaaaaank gaaaaank

rat - tat - tat - tat - tat

creet creet creet

shhhhhhhhhhhhhhhh

bzzzzzzzzzz

Outside, Inside

by Carolyn Crimi

Primary Lesson

Materials:

Outside, Inside, five large sheets of chart paper, five sticky notes for each student, marker, pencils, paper, writing folders or notebooks

Mini-lesson:

using specific verbs

Mini-lesson

A. Build background.

Ask the class if they ever look out the window when they are inside to see what is happening outside.

Have the class look out the classroom window. Ask them what they see happening outside the window. Lead them to notice that even though they are inside there are still many activities going on outside.

B. Introduce the book and author.

Tell the students the book tells the story of a girl just getting out of bed inside her house while a thunderstorm is brewing outside. Ask the class to listen for all the activities happening outside as the rain begins.

C. Read the book aloud.

D. Discuss the following.

Ask the class what the author told them about the rainstorm. Examples of student responses might include that it was raining, the wind was blowing, or it was thundering and lightning.

Explain that there are thousands of words that an author can choose from when writing. Authors can pick any word as long as it makes sense. Sometimes writers find a word they really like, or know how to spell, and they use it over and over again. They use it so much it gets tired. Then, the reader gets tired from reading the same word over and over.

Explain that good writers don't want that to happen, so they are always on the lookout for words that are different and exciting. Explain that verbs are the words that show the action in a story. Good writers use verbs that are strong, specific, and not tired.

Divide a sheet of chart paper in half vertically. On one side write *tired words*, and on the other side write *sparkle words*.

Reread this sentence from the book. *Outside, a worried rabbit darts across the lawn.* Hold the book where all students can see it.

Ask which word has the same meaning as *ran*. (*Darts.*) Write the word *ran* under the tired word side. Write the word *darts* under the sparkle word side. Point out that the author, Carolyn Crimi, chose a better word to describe how the rabbit got across the lawn.

Reread this sentence from the book. *Outside, tree leaves flap in the crying wind.* Again, hold the book so all can see the words.

Ask which word has the same meaning as *blow*. The answer is *flap*. Write the word *blow* under the tired word side. Write the word *flap* on the sparkle word side. Emphasize that the author chose to use a better word to describe how the leaves were blowing in the wind.

E. **Model the skill.**

Have the class make their own sparkle word charts. Write the word *good* at the top of a new sheet of chart paper. Next, write the sentence, *I had a _____ time at the park.*

Give each student a sticky note. Instruct them to think of a sparkle word for *good*. Model an example, like *fantastic* or *terrific*, by writing it on the sticky note and attaching it to the chart.

Have each student do the same using their own sparkle word for *good*. When all sticky notes are up, read the sentence with student examples. For example, if a student wrote *wonderful* on their sticky note, you would read, *I had a wonderful time at the park.* If there are duplicates, reread them anyway.

Repeat this activity using the following sentences:

The party was _____. Find a sparkle word for *fun*.

Mom _____ that it was time for dinner. Find a better word for *said*.

We _____ to the beach. Find a better word for *went*.

Return to the tired word/sparkle word chart from the beginning of the lesson. Add the words *fun, said,* and *went* to the tired word side. Choose one or two of the sticky notes with a better word choice for each word and add those words to the sparkle word side.

Quiet Writing/Conferencing

As students move into independent, quiet writing, remind them to think hard about the words they choose to use in their pieces. Encourage them not to use any of the tired words on the charts. If they are beginning new pieces and are considering using the words *good, fun, said, or went,* invite them to take a sticky note from the chart to help them use a sparkle word instead.

If they are continuing pieces of writing from a previous writing workshop, invite them to exchange their tired words for sparkle words.

During conferencing, you should point out tired words to the students and help them brainstorm words that would make their sentences sparkle.

Sharing

Choose two or three students to share their writing pieces. As students share, pick out the sparkle words and say, *I like the way you used the word* _____ *instead of* _____.

When sparkle words are used that are not on the chart from the mini-lesson, ask a volunteer to write the tired word on the chart, make a sticky note of the sparkle word, and add it there. You also can write the sparkle words on index cards with glitter glue so that they really do sparkle.

Outside, Inside

by Carolyn Crimi

Intermediate Lesson

Materials:

Outside, Inside, chart paper, markers, thesauri, students' notebooks and writing folders

Mini-lesson:

choosing specific verbs

Mini-lesson

A. Build background.

Review the definition of verbs as words that indicate action.

Tell students that today they will focus on choosing and using strong active verbs in their writing.

Discuss the difference between wimpy verbs and active verbs through the three examples on the chart which follows the Sharing section of the lesson.

Use the chart to read each pair of sentences aloud and discuss the differences in meaning. Identify and highlight the verbs in each sentence.

B. Introduce book and author.

Tell students that this book actually has two stories. One story happens outside a home, and the other happens inside the same home.

Tell students that many actions will occur in both stories. As they listen to the stories, they should jot down all the verbs they hear.

C. Read book aloud.

D. Discuss the following.

Explain the difference between wimpy verbs (passive and non-specific) and active verbs (clear and specific).

Look back at the highlighted verbs on the chart. Sort them into two lists, *Wimpy Verbs* and *Active Verbs.*

Tell students to look over their lists and share any wimpy verbs from the book. (There aren't any!)

Conclude with students that the author used only clear, specific verbs. Her book is full of active verbs.

Ask students to share some of the verbs they identified from the book. Add these active verbs to the list on the chart.

Add some other wimpy verbs to the list such as *make, do, said.*

To further emphasize the difference in meaning and effectiveness, try reading a few pages from the book by substituting wimpy verbs.

If students are not familiar with using a thesaurus, introduce how to use this reference. Demonstrate by looking up wimpy verbs and finding synonyms.

Explain to students that a thesaurus is a tool writers use to help improve word choice.

Guide students to conclude that active verbs paint clear, meaningful pictures in the reader's mind. A thesaurus can assist them with substituting active verbs for wimpy verbs.

Tell students that active verbs are especially useful in narrative writing for describing events and characters' actions. They may also be effectively used in expository writing such as in describing animal behavior, a weather occurrence, or an historical event.

Quiet Writing/Conferencing

Tell students that to practice using active verbs they will begin with planning and composing an expository piece. Ask students to think about something they like to do. Have them make jot lists of verbs to describe all the actions in the activity. Then have students write paragraphs using active verbs that describe themselves involved in the activity.

Have students practice this skill in narrative writing by choosing older pieces in their writing folder to work on. The pieces may be in draft or finished form. Ask the students to read through the pieces and highlight all the verbs. Then have the students decide which verbs are passive or wimpy, and how they could improve them.

Sharing

As students share their pieces, have the class note active verbs that are used in the writing. If the student is sharing an older piece of writing with revised verbs, have the student read the old version first and then the new one so the class can appreciate the difference in meaning. After each student shares a piece, invite the class to ask questions and offer comments.

Chart

Intermediate Lesson
for
Outside, Inside

1. After school I will <u>play</u> with my friends. (wimpy verb)

   After school I will <u>glide</u> on my skateboard, <u>shoot</u> some hoops, and <u>climb</u> trees with my friends. (active verbs)

2. I <u>went</u> to the park. (wimpy verb)

   I <u>rode</u> my bicycle to the park. (active verb)

3. I <u>will get</u> a birthday present for my friend. (wimpy verb)

   I <u>will go shopping</u> and <u>choose</u> a birthday present for my friend. (active verbs)

Wimpy Verbs	Active Verbs	
play	glide	slips
went	shoot	scratches
will get	climb	streaks
make	rode	rushes
do	will go shopping	skim
said	choose	stomps
	sink	twirls
	stretches	slows
	yawns	counts
	flap	rolling
	whisper	squishes
	darts	shakes
	sleeps	arches
	spills	pushes
	ticks	swings
	bubble	lets
	churn	

Alexander and the Terrible, Horrible, No Good, Very Bad Day

by Judith Viorst

Primary Lesson

Materials:

Alexander and the Terrible, Horrible, No Good, Very Bad Day, chart paper, marker, paper, pencils, writing folder or notebook.

Mini-lesson:

descriptive language

NOTE:

Webs are not developmentally appropriate for narrative pieces with K-2 students.

Mini-lesson

A. Build background.

Ask students to think back to days when nothing seemed to go right. Ask a few to briefly share their bad days.

B. Introduce the book and the author.

Ask students to predict what kind of day the character, Alexander, probably had in the book.

Ask them to listen as the book is read for reasons why the day was so terrible, horrible, and very bad.

C. Read the book aloud.

D. Discuss the following.

Write the words *horrible, terrible, no good, very bad* as a heading at the top of a sheet of chart paper. Draw a series of separate boxes with an arrowed line between each. An example of a graphic organizer can be found behind the Sharing section of this lesson.

Ask what happened first that made Alexander think it was going to be a bad day. Write the reason in the first box.

Ask what happened at breakfast that was horrible. Write the answer in the next box.

Ask what happened in the car pool that was very bad. Write the answer in the next box.

Ask what happened at lunch that was terrible. Write the answer in the next box.

Ask what happened at the dentist. Write the answer in the fifth box.

Finally, ask what happened at the shoe store that was no good, and write the answer in the last box.

E. Model the skill.

Explain to the class they have just constructed a graphic organizer. Writers use organizers to organize their thoughts. All the examples written in the boxes show the reader how terrible, horrible, no good, and very bad Alexander's day was.

The author didn't just tell the reader Alexander had a bad day. She used specific examples to show the reader. This is called descriptive language.

Put a clean sheet of chart paper up. Write the words *terrific, wonderful,* and *very good* as a heading. Draw six boxes, as before.

Ask students to brainstorm examples of terrific, wonderful, very good things they have experienced. As students share, choose six examples and write them in the boxes, in chronological order.

Explain that they have made a graphic organizer. This organizer could be used to write a few sentences or a paragraph about a terrific, wonderful, very good day.

Quiet Writing/Conferencing

Give each student a blank sheet of paper. Guide them in writing a lead sentence that reads, *I knew it was going to be a terrific, wonderful, very good day when.......*

Teachers of emergent writers can pre-print a lead on sheets of paper for each students. In this case, you should model how to take one box and turn it into a sentence. For example, if one box reads, *I got a new bike,* you would write, *I knew it was going to be terrific, wonderful, very good day when I got a new, black, mountain bike with wide tires from my grandpa.* Teachers of emergent writers simply can write, *I got a new red bike.*

Explain that specific details, like the color of the bike or the size of the tires, make the sentences more descriptive.

Ask students to write a description of a very good day using the graphic organizer. Emergent writers may write only a few words. Developing writers will write more than one sentence. Encourage them to add more details to what is written in the box. Refer students back to your model to observe the extra details added about the bike. After five to ten minutes, have volunteers share what they have written about their terrific, wonderful, very good day.

Send students to independent quiet writing with the choice of continuing the *good day* piece or an older piece. You can also ask them to choose new topics, construct graphic organizers, and write descriptive sentences. Note that the organizers they construct may not have exactly six boxes.

Sharing

Ask three students to share. Have them show their organizers before they read their pieces. Ask students to tell the audience how the organizers helped organize their pieces. Note examples of descriptive language which were added to enhance the description in the box.

Graphic Organizer

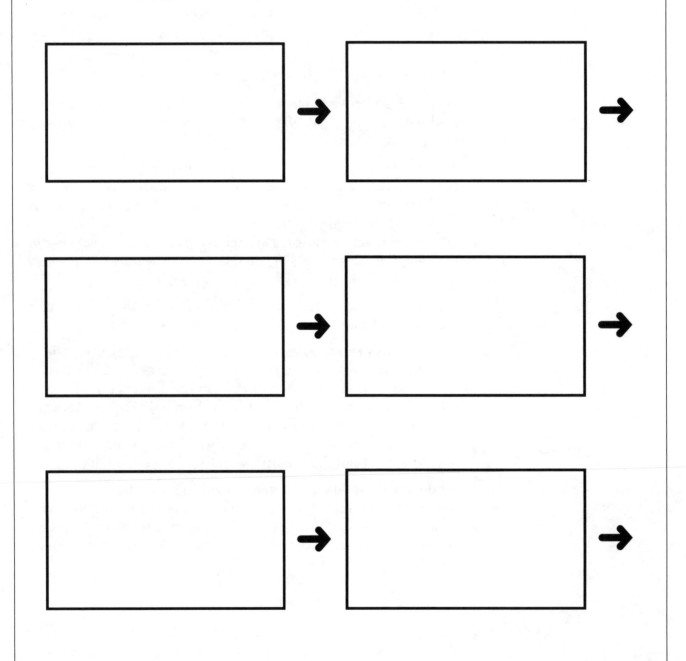

Alexander and the Terrible, Horrible, No Good, Very Bad Day

by Judith Viorst

Intermediate Lesson

Materials:

Alexander and the Terrible, Horrible, No Good, Very Bad Day, chart paper, markers, thesauri, students' notebooks and writing folders.

Mini-lesson:

using a thesaurus to develop descriptive language

Mini-lesson

A. Build background.

Ask students to recall a time when they experienced bad days. It may have been a time when one major bad thing happened or a time when a series of little things just didn't go well.

Share a few responses, and note which examples related a series of events that did not turn out well.

B. Introduce book and author.

Tell students to make predictions about the character, Alexander, based on the title. Invite them to jot down some of the things that happen to Alexander in this book, especially ones that have happened to them as well.

C. Read book aloud.

D. Discuss the following.

Ask students why they think Judith Viorst gave the book this title.

Ask students to recall some of the things that happened to Alexander. As students share responses, invite them to tell if any of these events ever happened to them.

Ask students if they noticed a pattern in how the author used the title of the book in the story. (They should note the repeating line, *It was a terrible, horrible, no good, very bad day.*)

Discuss with students how the many examples of unhappy events followed by the repeating line allowed the reader to see what a bad day Alexander was having. If the author had merely written *bad day*, readers would not gather the full meaning of such an awful day.

E. Introduce the thesaurus.

Tell students that writers often do not want to repeat the same words over and over, so they try to come up with different words that mean the same thing.

A thesaurus is a reference book that offers a great deal of help with finding descriptive words that are similar to one another. Write the word *horrible* on chart paper.

Demonstrate how to use the thesaurus by looking up the word *horrible*. Read aloud some synonyms for this word such as *frightful, shocking, unpleasant,* and *ugly*. Write these under the word *horrible*. Note that Judith Viorst also used *terrible, no good,* and *very bad,* as synonyms for *horrible*.

Model using the thesaurus for the word *bad*. Write this word in a second column. Look up the word in the thesaurus, and list some synonyms. You may wish to show one or two examples for more positive words, such as *happy*. See the chart example which follows the Sharing section.

In conclusion, tell students that using a thesaurus to add descriptive language is another writers' tool for developing elaboration skills.

Quiet Writing/Conferencing

Ask students to think again about the time they had bad days or times they had wonderful days. Direct students to plan the big ideas of what happened that day for narrative pieces of writing. Sometimes students may feel that they don't have enough information to write about a bad day. Perhaps only one or two things in a day did not go as planned. Encourage students to use fiction here. This gives them the freedom to combine non-fiction and fiction to create narrative pieces about truly bad days.

You may wish to encourage students to continue developing these narrative pieces over the next few days by asking them to add supporting ideas and details to the big ideas. Encourage students to use a thesaurus to help them with their word choices. Follow with composing a lead and ending. Refer to the Narrative Planning Sheet found at the end of this section of lessons. To complete the writing process, encourage students to spend time revising, editing, and publishing.

This topic also may be approached through expository writing. Ask students to think about a time they had a bad day or a wonderful day. What were the reasons the day did not turn out as they hoped, or what were the reasons the day was so wonderful? Consult the Expository Planning Sheet found at the end of this section.

Students may begin by planning to explain two or three reasons they had bad or wonderful days. Then they should work on the elaboration of each reason. Help students develop a lead and an ending to complete the first draft. As with the narrative suggestion described above, proceed with the next stages of the writing process by revising, editing, and publishing.

Encourage students to revisit other narrative and expository pieces in their folders to add or improve elaborative details.

Sharing

As students share, model how to ask questions and offer comments about the pieces of writing. Invite the students to do the same. As each student shares a piece, have the class make note of which words especially describe a terrible day.

One question that inevitably will come up is whether the piece is fiction or non-fiction. Many writers will probably say that parts of their pieces are non-fiction and parts are fiction. This will give you another opportunity to comment on how writers frequently get their ideas for books from little things that happen in real life.

An important question that you should ask of the writer is where they plan to go with the piece. This will help the writer begin rehearsing and planning for the next step in the piece of writing. This question also will nudge the rest of the class to do the same.

Encourage students to share other pieces of writing which reflect attention to elaboration skills. Have them read the pieces or parts of the pieces in their original forms, then in the revised forms. Direct the class to listen for the differences. Questions and comments should focus on the improved elaborations.

Chart

Intermediate Lesson
for
Alexander and the Terrible, Horrible, No Good, Very Bad Day

horrible	bad	happy
frightful	evil	pleasure
shocking	wicked	joyful
unpleasant	defective	contented
ugly	worthless	good luck
terrible	faulty	glad
no good	incorrect	delighted
very bad	rotten	cheerful

Owl Moon

by Jane Yolen

Primary Lesson

Materials:

Owl Moon, chart paper, marker, sentence strip for teacher, sentence strip for every student, pocket chart, writing folders, or notebooks, paper, pencils.

Mini-lesson:

descriptive language

Mini-lesson

A. Build background.

Ask students to share names of places they sometimes go with grown-ups. Examples might include the grocery store the bank, movies, etc. Ask if they had to wait until they got to a certain age to go to some of those places. Have a few students share. Ask if any member of the class has ever gone owling.

B. Introduce the book and the author.

Show the cover of the book. Point out the child and the adult. Ask for a prediction as to who they might be.

Explain the characters on the cover are about to do something the child has been looking forward to for a long time. They are going owling.

Explain that because owling is such an unusual activity that most children know nothing about it. One way to learning about owling is to listen closely to the book.

C. Read the book aloud.

D. Discuss the following.

Have several students explain what they now know about owling. Explain that the author used wonderful, descriptive words to show what a special activity owling really is.

E. Model the skill.

Ask the class to answer the following questions. Record their answers on a large piece of chart paper.

When did the child and the father go owling?
How did the child and the father get to the owling spot?
Was it warm or cold when the child and the father went owling?
Did the owl answer when the father called it?
What is the one thing you need when you go owling?

The students' answers will probably be one or two words. For example, the answer to the first question will probably be *at night* or *in the winter*. (You should write on the chart, *They went owling at night.*)

The answer to the second question will probably be *They walked.* Write on the chart, *They walked.*

Continue recording the rest of the student answers.

Go over the student answers. Then reread the first page of the book. Have students listen for the words the author used to tell the reader when the child and his father went owling.

Ask if there was more information on the page than *It was night*. Ask for a few volunteers to share what information they heard.

Reread page four of the book. Ask if the author gave the reader more information than *They walked*. Ask for a few volunteers to share what they heard that was more than just *They walked*.

Reread page ten and ask the class to use the text they just heard to share more information about how cold it was.

Reread page seventeen and ask students if they can tell from the description if the owl answered back immediately.

Read the last page. Ask the class what they thought the author meant by the word *hope*.

Quiet Writing/Conferencing

Note the differences between the written answers on the chart paper and the words written in the book. The author used special words and details that made owling so vivid and real that the readers felt like they were there, too. That is called descriptive language.

On a sentence strip, write the sentence, *It was early in the morning when.....* Ask students to share activities that happen early in the morning at their house.

Give each student a sentence strip. Have the class choose one of those activities and write it on their personal sentence strips. Go around the room and have each student share their example, preceded by *It was early in the morning when...* (Examples might be... *It was early in the morning when I got out of bed,* or *It was early in the morning when I ate my breakfast.*)

Have two students put their sentence strips under the teacher strip that reads, *It was early in the morning when...*

Have those students stand in front of the room while the rest of the class asks specific questions about their event. For example, if the event was *I ate my breakfast*, the class should ask questions such as,

> *What did you have for breakfast?*
> *Where were you when you ate your breakfast?*
> *How did your breakfast taste?*

Explain that writing becomes more descriptive as more details about the morning event are shared.

Next ask students which story would be more descriptive: the one that reads *It was early in the morning when I ate breakfast,* or *It was early in the morning when I sat down at my kitchen table to eat my steaming hot pancakes.*

Discuss which words make the sentence more descriptive.

As students move to independent, quiet writing, encourage them to try putting details in all their pieces to make their writing more descriptive. Give them the choice of beginning their own pieces about the early morning or to choose other topics.

As you conference, prompt students to show the reader specific details, not just to tell what happened. *Show, don't tell* means the writer makes readers feel as though they were watching the event unfold or experiencing it themselves, rather than simply being told what happened. For example, if students are writing narrative pieces about how happy they felt at their birthday parties, encourage them to help the reader to see and feel the happiness.

Sharing

During sharing, have students reread any descriptive language found in their pieces. Model how to compare sentences with descriptive language and those without by saying, *I noticed you wrote, 'My legs were shaking and my hands were sweating,' instead of simply writing, 'I was scared'.*

Owl Moon

by Jane Yolen

Intermediate Lesson

Materials:

Owl Moon, chart or transparency of the chart, chart paper, markers, students' notebooks and writing folders.

Mini-lesson:

descriptive language

Mini-lesson

A. Build background.

Ask students to remember times when they had to wait a long time to do something. Tell them to try to recall the anticipation of doing whatever they had waited so long to do. Have a few students share what they waited to do.

Ask students to remember what it was actually like when that moment happened. How did they feel? What did they think? How did they act?

B. Introduce book title and author.

Ask students to make predictions about the book. Explain to students that in this story a young girl has the chance to do something she has looked forward to for a long time.

Tell students to notice the details she uses to describe her experience and to jot down those they find especially descriptive.

C. Read book aloud.

D. Discuss the following.

Ask students how the title of this book matches the story. Invite students to share some of the details they noted on their papers. Discuss which part of the story the details described.

Refer to the chart which follows the Sharing section of the lesson. Discuss the places Jane Yolen used a type of comparison known as simile.

Discuss the examples where the author used *as if* to illustrate the meaning.

Refer to the chart to discuss other items that were beautifully described.

Show students how different this story would have been if Jane Yolen had not used so many descriptive details. Read some of the phrases in the chart without the details. Invite students to comment on the difference in meaning. Summarize by telling students that it is their choice of words and skill in combining words which determines the message imprinted on the reader. Explain that writers are like artists, using words instead of paint to create a picture. Writers choose details that turn their writing into anything they wish it to be.

Quiet Writing/Conferencing

Ask students to think again about times they looked forward to doing something and how good it felt to be able to do it at last. Consult the form for planning and developing a narrative piece of writing at the end of this section. Ask students to begin planning the big ideas, supporting ideas, and details describing this event in narrative form. You may wish to have students continue writing on this topic for several days.

After students plan the big ideas of the narrative, they will need to compose a lead and ending. Once they complete their first drafts, students should spend time revising and editing their pieces and decide whether to publish them.

Encourage students to work on adding elaboration to other narrative and expository pieces in their folders. Remind them to think about ways to use elaboration effectively as Jane Yolen did.

Sharing

As each student shares a piece, remind the class how to ask questions and offer comments effectively. Ask the class to make notes of outstanding details and to let the writer know how effective those words were. If this is the first day of working on the topic, ask a writer where he plans to go with the piece of writing. This question prompts all students to rehearse for the next writing workshop.

Invite students to share examples of revised elaboration from other pieces. Have them read the first drafts, then the second drafts or revised portions. A powerful question to ask is, *What made you decide to make that revision?* The students will share their own think-aloud processes that enabled them to revise. This is the best model for other students. It also empowers writers by helping them realize that they are in charge of their writing!

Chart

Intermediate Lesson
for
Owl Moon

(Use all or parts of this on chart paper or overhead transparency.)

Description by simile

The trees stood still as giant statues.

Somewhere behind us a train whistle blew, long and low, like a sad, sad song.

And when their voices faded away it was as quiet as a dream.

Then the owl pumped its great wings and lifted off the branch like a shadow without sound.

Descriptions using *As if*

He looked up, as if searching the stars, as if reading a map up there.

I could feel the cold, as if someone's icy hand was palm-down on my back.

Pa almost smiled. Then he called back: "Whoo-whoo-who-who-who-whoooooooo," just as if he and the owl were talking about supper or about the woods or the moon or the cold.

Other Descriptive Language

It was late one winter night, long past my bedtime when Pa and I went owling.

Our feet crunched over the crisp snow and little gray footprints followed us.

Pa made a long shadow, but mine was short and round....my short, round shadow bumped after me.

We reached the line of pine trees, black and pointy against the sky...

The moon made his face into a silver mask.

And my nose and the tops of my cheeks felt cold and hot at the same time.

The shadows were the blackest things I had ever seen. They stained the white snow.

My mouth felt furry, for the scarf over it was wet and warm.

(The moon) seemed to fit exactly over the center of the clearing and the snow below it was whiter than the milk in a cereal bowl.

I listened and looked so hard my ears hurt and my eyes got cloudy with the cold.

For one minute, three minutes, maybe even a hundred minutes, we stared at one another.

Expository Planning Sheet

Five Paragraphs

Paragraph #1 Lead with two sentences

- Share a feeling about the topic, or ask the reader a question about the topic.
- Write the topic.

Paragraph #2 First reason or step, or
First part of description

- Write 1 Big Idea beginning with a transition word.
- Write 1-2 Supporting Ideas which tell more about the Big Idea.
- Write 3-4 Details using elaboration skills.

Paragraph #3 Second reason or step, or
Second part of description

- Write 1 Big Idea beginning with a transition word.
- Write 1-2 Supporting Ideas which tell more about the Big Idea.
- Write 3-4 Details using elaboration skills.

Paragraph #4 Third reason or step, or
Third part of description

- Write 1 Big Idea beginning with a transition word.
- Write 1-2 Supporting Ideas which tell more about the Big Idea.
- Write 3-4 Details using elaboration skills.

Paragraph #5 Ending with 2 sentences

- Restate the topic.
- Share a feeling about the topic or give advice to the reader about the topic.

Narrative Planning Sheet

Five Paragraphs

Paragraph #1 Lead with three sentences

- Describe the time and place.
- Describe the character.
- State the topic.

Paragraph #2 First Part of the Story

- Describe what happened right before the main part of the story.
- What happens to the character that results in a problem to solve or a goal to achieve?

Paragraph #3 Second Part of the Story

- Describe the main part of the story. How was the problem solved? How was the goal achieved?
- Tell the events in chronological order.
- Use transition words such as *first, next, then, after,* and *finally.*

Paragraph #4 Third Part of the Story

- Describe what happened right after the problem was solved or goal was achieved.
- Describe the solution to the problem or the achievement of the goal.

Paragraph #5 Ending with two sentences

- Restate the topic.
- Share a feeling about the topic, or give advice to the reader about the topic.

CHAPTER FOUR

Organization

By the time students are ready to learn about and use transition words, they will feel successful with the planning and composing stages of writing. They now have a body of writing that requires a strategy for organizing the main ideas. For writing purposes, transition words signal the changing of one idea to the next in both expository and narrative text. Transition words help the reader connect the meaning of one part of text to another.

Writers frequently use transition words when they relate information about a topic. The writer may explain something, such as how to feed a pet. Transition words similar to first, next, and finally help to move the text along. Expository text that describes a topic may outline certain characteristics of that topic. For example, a writer may describe a pet and choose to elaborate on two or three of its characteristics. Transition words are used to move from one characteristic to another.

Narrative writing must contain transition words so the reader can understand how events happen in a chronological order. Transition words in narrative writing signal the passage of time. For example, consider a typical fairy tale. It begins with *Once upon a time...* and ends with *...happily ever after*. The words *once* and *after* tell the reader that the story is beginning or ending. When students relate their own narratives, they search for ways to begin the story, then move to the middle, and finally the conclusion. Examples of narrative transition words and phrases may include *today, tomorrow, yesterday, before, later, in the morning*, or *after a while*.

Introduce transition words to students as signal words. They signal a change in the piece of writing. The lessons in this section use narrative books as models, but some of the examples of transition words may be used for expository writing as well.

You will need to decide when and where to expect your students to use transition words. In kindergarten, students may write about little accidents they had and tell what happened first and next. In first grade, students may learn to write expository or narrative pieces with a simple beginning, middle, and end. For example, if first graders are writing about a favorite place and the reasons this place is so special, they can begin each reason with *My first reason...* and *My last*, or, *My next reason*.

Transition words often serve as signals to begin new paragraphs. Although kindergarten, first- and second-grade students will use transitions in their speaking vocabulary and written language, they are generally not developmentally ready to indent new paragraphs. Third-grade students are developmentally able to transfer the concept of new ideas to new paragraphs on their paper. The use of transition words at the beginning of each new big idea will enable most third graders to master the skill of paragraphing narrative and expository information.

In the intermediate grades, you can refer to the non-fiction texts found in science and social studies books to develop the skill of transition. For example, fourth- and fifth-grade students learn how to organize information in outline form. They could write a summarizing paragraph about each section of an outline. Each paragraph would begin with a transition word such as *The first section of this chapter is about...*

You may have students write about field trips to practice the use of transition words. Ask students, *What did we do first?* List the big ideas of the trip on chart paper, and have the class write pieces about the trip.

Two other books to use for teaching transition words:

Fireflies by Julie Brinckloe
Rosie's Walk by Pat Hutchins

Ira Sleeps Over

by Bernard Weber

Primary Lesson

Materials:

Ira Sleeps Over, chart paper divided horizontally into three sections, black marker, three different colored transparency markers, Transparency One, three different colored dots

Mini-lesson:

beginning, middle, and end

Mini-lesson

A. Build background.

Divide a large sheet of chart paper horizontally into three sections. Write *Lunch* at the top of the chart. Write *Beginning* in the first section, *Middle* in the middle section, and *End* in the last section.

Ask students to brainstorm all the activities that occur before, during, and after lunch time at school. As the students give examples, ask them to determine when the activity occurs. Does it happen at the beginning of the lunch period, during the middle of the lunch period, or at the end?

Write the student suggestions on the chart in the appropriate section. For example, *Wash hands* would be written in the first section. *Eat my sandwich* would be written in the middle section, and *Throw trash away* would be written in the last section.

Reread the chart after all suggestions have been added. Ask why each activity was written in the section it was. Determine that it wouldn't make sense to put *Wash hands* in the last section because hands are not washed last. *Eat my sandwich* doesn't go at the end of lunch because that is not when it happens.

Explain that putting all the lunch period activities in the order that they happened organizes the piece. That is the only way understanding what happens during lunch will make sense.

Explain that for any piece of writing to make sense it also must have a beginning, middle, and an end.

B. Introduce the book and the author.

Explain that Ira, the little boy in the book, is invited to spend the night at a friend's house. In the beginning of the book, he is nervous about taking his teddy bear with him. He is afraid his friend will laugh at him. He asks for advice from his family about taking his bear. Finally, in the end he must make his own decision whether to take the bear or not.

C. Read the book aloud.

D. Discuss the following.

What happened in the beginning of the story that made Ira decide not to take his bear with him?

What happened in the middle of the story that made Ira decide to take his bear with him?

What happened at the end of the story to make Ira go back home and get his bear?

E. Model the skill.

Show Transparency One found following the Sharing section of this lesson. Tell the students they are going to help determine where in the story each sentence would be found. Use three different colored markers to underline the sentences. For example, if the sentence is found at the beginning of the book, underline it in red. If the sentence is found in the middle of the book, underline it in blue, and if it is found at the end, underline it in green.

Read each sentence and ask for a volunteer to underline it in the correct color. Ask the volunteer to explain his choice of color. Restate each time that organizing the writing is very important for the story to make sense.

Quiet Writing/Conferencing

Give each student three colored dots to match the colored markers used in modeling the skill.

Ask students to think about their writing topics they have chosen for the day. It may be about their own special items that they sleep with. It may be about sleepovers they have experienced, or it may be about a topic that has nothing to do with the book just read. Whatever the topics, ask students to think about what will happen in the beginning, the middle, and the end of the piece. After one to two minutes, send them to individual, quiet writing.

After ten minutes of quiet writing, ask students to place the stickers symbolizing the beginning in the margin next to the beginning of their pieces. Ask them to place their stickers for the middle in the margin next to the middle of the piece. Do the same with the ending. Tell students who have not completed their pieces to save and place the stickers after they finish.

Circulate, and note where the stickers are placed. Help students to see where sentences may be moved for clarity, and help them move the stickers to the appropriate place if necessary. Review the concept that good pieces of writing have a clear beginning, middle, and end.

Sharing

Ask students to read sections of their pieces in the wrong order purposely. For example, have them reread the beginning and the end in reverse order. Ask students if the piece makes sense. Then ask the reader to reread the piece in the correct order. Note the difference in clarity.

Transparency One

Primary Lesson
for
Ira Sleeps Over

I went next door where Reggie lived.

I was invited to sleep at Reggie's house.

"Good night," I whispered to Tah Tah.

That night, Reggie showed me his junk collection.

I will probably love sleeping without my teddy bear.

Reggie began to tell a ghost story.

I decided not to take my teddy bear.

Reggie was fast asleep.

At last, it was time to go to Reggie's.

Ira Sleeps Over

by Bernard Waber

Intermediate Lesson

Materials:

Ira Sleeps Over, chart paper, black, blue, green, and red markers, students' notebooks, and writing folders.

Mini-lesson:

beginning, middle, and end; transition words

Mini-lesson

A. Build background.

Ask students to think of the first time they spent a night at another person's house. It may have been a relative or friend's house, or a camping trip with Scouts. Share a few responses.

Ask the students if they have special possessions that go with them when they spend the night away from home. Share a few responses.

B. Introduce book and author.

Tell students that spending the night away from home is a big event, especially the first time. For some people, it's a lot of fun to plan, but for others it may be a little scary to be away from home.

Explain to students that Ira is excited about spending the night at his friend's house, but he's also worried. Tell them that the story takes place in one day, and they should notice all the things that happen to Ira from morning to night.

C. Read book aloud.

D. Discuss the following.

Ask students if they felt the way Ira did when they spent their first night away from home. Share a few responses.

Ask students to think back to the beginning of the story and recall the events that happened. Record their responses on chart paper. Continue probing with the question: *And then what happened?*

When students have retold the events, look over the chart. Using the black marker, number them in order.

Review the events and discuss which ones happened at the beginning of the story, which ones happened in the middle, and which occured at the end. Label each beginning statement with a green A, each middle statement with a blue B, and each ending statement with a red C.

Discuss the fact that although the blue, or middle story statements, have the most elaboration, all three parts are necessary to a complete narrative. Ask students how they knew the order of the events. Discuss the importance of transition words. Tell students that authors use transition words so readers can understand the order of the events and can make sense of the story.

Skim through the pages of the book, and locate the transition words used by Bernard Waber. Refer to the chart which follows the Sharing portion.

Choose a few of these pages, and reread them without the transition words. Guide students to conclude that transition words have an important part in helping readers gather meaning from a story.

Generate a class list of frequently used transition words. See examples on the chart.

Quiet Writing/Conferencing

A good way to practice using transition words that show the passage of time is to think of activities that every student can respond to, such as getting ready for school. Have students make jot lists of the things they do to get ready for school and ask them to number these in sequence. As they write these events in a paragraph, students will find that they need to insert transition words.

Begin with a simple exercise, such as asking students to explain how to make their beds, tie their shoelaces, or do simple chores around the house. Students will use transition words, such as *first, second, next,* and *finally.*

Choosing topics that require students to give reasons why or why not is another way to demonstrate the use of transition words in expository writing. For example: *Why do you like to eat pizza?* You can ask students to use transition words to begin every reason, such as *My first reason, The next reason,* etc. Finally, you may find examples of transition words in science texts, especially in activity or experiment lessons.

Sharing

As students share their pieces, have the class make notes of transition words that are used. You may consider asking several students to read pieces with transition words and then without them. Have the class comment on the difference in meaning.

Chart

Intermediate Lesson
for
Ira Sleeps Over

p. 3   I had never slept at a friend's house before.

p. 4   It began...

p. 6   And then...

p. 10   But now...
Now...
I began...

p. 16   That afternoon...
Tonight...
First...
And after that...
And after that...
And after that...
And after that...
And after that...
And after that...

p. 18   And after that...
I began...

p. 20   Suddenly...

p.26   At last, it was time to go...

p. 28   That night...

p. 30   After that...
And after that...

p. 31   And after that...

p. 35   Reggie began...

p. 39   Just a minute...

p. 40   The next minute...

p. 42   Soon...

p. 48   And after that...

Chart

Intermediate Lesson
for
Ira Sleeps Over

Examples of Transition Words

about

after, afterwards

after two hours

a week passed

at that moment

before

during

finally

first

immediately

in a few minutes

last week

later

meanwhile

next

next day, next month, next Saturday

second, secondly

soon

then

today

tomorrow

until

yesterday

Comet's Nine Lives

by Jan Brett

Primary Lesson

Materials:

Comet's Nine Lives, transparency and/or individual copies of Morning Job Flowchart for each student, blank sheet of paper for each student, chart of transition words for teacher reference, chart paper, marker, writing folder or notebook, pencils.

Mini-lesson:

transition words

Mini-lesson

A. **Build background.**

Discuss the concept of a routine.

Explain that doing a group of activities in the same order time after time is called a routine.

Use the example of the morning classroom routine. Make a transparency of the flowchart found after the Sharing section of this lesson. Students should have their own blank copies to fill in as well. (Note: Kindergarten teachers may choose to do this as a whole-group activity with only the teacher doing the writing.)

Ask students to share what they do first every day when they enter the classroom. Write it in Box One.

Ask what they do second; write it in Box Two.

Continue this procedure until all boxes are filled. Put the flow-chart aside until the Model the Skill section of this lesson.

B. **Introduce the book and author.**

Explain that the book is the story of a cat who has quite a series of events happen to him while he searches for a home. Ask the students to listen for what happens to Comet first, second, third and so on.

C. **Read the book aloud.**

D. **Discuss the following.**

Ask what happened to poor Comet that took away his first life. (Comet ate foxgloves.)

Ask what happened second that took away one of poor Comet's lives. (A pile of bestsellers toppled on Comet.)

Ask what happened to Comet next. (Comet fell out of the boat at sea.)

Continue this pattern until you have reviewed all eight events that took nearly all of Comet's nine lives. Use the pictures in the book to help students recollect the events.

E. **Introduce transition words.**

Ask students if they think the author, Jan Brett, wanted the reader to know each time Comet lost a life. (Yes, she did.) She did this by using special words called *transition words* that let readers know each time a new event began. Transition words are words like *first, second, third, fourth, next, then,* or *finally.*

Write these words on a piece of chart paper, and point to them as you say them aloud. If students can add a transition word to the list, write their words on the chart as well. A list of transition words can be found following the Sharing section of this lesson. Any of these words could be put on the chart.

Review the idea that transition words help put a piece of writing in correct order, helping it to make sense.

F. **Reread pages two and three.**

Have students identify the transition words. (They are *first, then,* and *when.*)

Reread pages two and three without the transition words, allowing students to hear the difference.

Reread several more pages. Have students identify the transition word on each page. Reread the page without the transition words to allow students to hear the difference.

G. **Model the skill.**

Have students refer to the flow chart of their morning routines. Reread the activities written in the boxes.

Review the transition words on the class-made chart. Tell students they are going to use transition words with the flowchart to tie their morning routine together.

The teacher and student write *first* on top of the first box of the flowchart. (Note: Kindergarten teachers who choose to do the flow chart activity in a whole group will need to do this portion of the lesson that way as well.)

Write *second* on top of the second box.

Continue to the next boxes writing the words *third, next,* and *finally* respectively above each box.

Give each student a blank sheet of paper. Take each box and model how to turn it into a sentence. For example, if in the first box of the flow-chart, *hand in homework* is written, the teacher models writing, *First, I hand in my homework.*

Have each student write the sentence on a piece of paper. Kindergarten students who are unable to write independently will benefit from watching the teacher model. For the second box on the flow chart, encourage students to independently try to match the transition word with the phrase in the box to make a sentence. For example, if in the second box, *sharpen pencil* is written, the student should write, *Second, I sharpen my pencil.* Once again, kindergarten students can verbalize how to match the transition word while you do the writing.

Continue until all boxes have been converted into sentences. Explain that now these sentences can be put together to form a piece about how a day in the classroom begins.

Quiet Writing/Conferencing

As students move into independent, quiet writing, encourage them to rewrite their pieces independently about the morning routines. Kindergarten students should be able to attempt writing a sentence with a transition word now.

Remind older students they will need a beginning and ending sentence to tie their pieces about the morning routine together. If students are not familiar with writing leads and endings, these would make excellent mini-lessons for future writing workshops.

Students also should be given the choice of beginning new pieces of writing. Remind them to use transitions words to move their writing forward. Have extra blank flowcharts available to use with their new pieces.

Sharing

Ask two or three students to share their pieces about morning routines. Ask students to listen for transition words, repeating them back to the author, beginning the sentences with *I heard you used the transition word......*

Have one student share a new piece of writing. Ask the others to listen for transition words, then repeat them back to the author.

Leave the transition-word chart up for students to refer to during future writing workshops.

Morning Job Flowchart

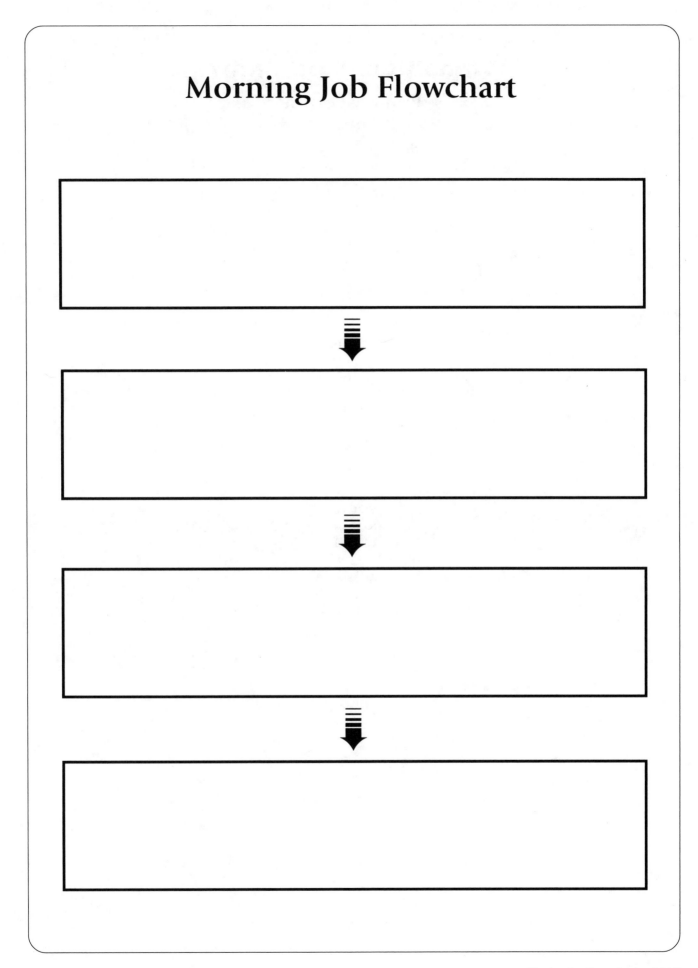

Transition Word Chart

Primary Lesson
for
Comet's Nine Lives

after

before

first

second

third

fourth

last

later

soon

when

until

meanwhile

before

today

tomorrow

Comet's Nine Lives

by Jan Brett

Intermediate Lesson

Materials:

Comet's Nine Lives, chart paper, markers, students' notebooks, and writing folders

Mini-lesson:

transition words

Mini-lesson

A. Build background.

Discuss with students that readers need to hear or read thoughts in an order that makes sense if they are to understand information in expository writing or events in narrative writing.

In expository writing, an author describes or explains one idea at a time, creating order and clear meaning for the reader.

In narrative writing, an author describes events in an order revealing to the reader that time is passing by.

Tell students that in both expository and narrative writing, writers need to learn the skill of moving from one part of a piece of writing to another. Today they will concentrate on how to do this in narrative writing.

Ask students to think of some words that show the passage of time. Share some responses.

B. Introduce book and author.

Ask students if they are familiar with the saying, *A cat has nine lives.* Clarify the meaning of this statement.

Explain to students that Jan Brett's artwork has many details. Some also are clues about what will happen in the story. Tell students that Comet, the cat, is the main character. His story unfolds over several months.

Tell students that they should listen for words that show time is passing by and jot these down on their papers.

C. Read book aloud.

D. Discuss the following.

Use the book's pictures as prompts. Have students retell the sequence of events in *Comet's Nine Lives.*

Ask students for examples of time words they jotted down. Record these on chart paper, such as on the sample chart found after the Sharing portion of this lesson.

Tell students that these words are transition words. They serve as a transition, or a bridge between one thought and another by telling the reader that time is passing by.

Go back to the beginning of the book. Help students identify all the transition words used in the book. Add new ones to the list. A complete list is given on the sample chart.

Ask students what would happen to the meaning of Jan Brett's story if none of the transition words were included. You may need to read a few pages without the transition words to demonstrate the loss of meaning in the story.

Quiet Writing/Conferencing

Tell students that people have all sorts of problems to solve every day, just as Comet had many little problems to solve before he could find a solution to his main problem. Ask students to think about times they had to solve problems.

Tell students that they will use this time to plan narrative pieces. They will need to consider where to use transition words to show the passing of time. Note that students will need several days to finish this piece if they follow through with all parts of the writing process.

Have students revisit other narrative pieces in their folders and look for transition words. Ask students to highlight transition words every time they find one. This helps students figure out where to insert other needed transition words in their own pieces.

Refer to the narrative and expository planning forms found at the end of the Elaboration section. Encourage students to use transition words at the beginning of every paragraph for both types of writing.

Finally, ask students to look for transition words in their science or social studies books, as well as the trade books or novels they are reading. This emphasizes how important these words are in any type of writing.

Sharing

As each student shares a piece, ask the class to listen for and comment on the use of transition words.

Chart
Intermediate Lesson
for
Comet's Nine Lives

<u>Transition words in text order</u>

first

then

until

just as

once

night

the next day

all too soon

fall

now

at that moment

winter

CHAPTER FIVE

Conventions of Language

The term conventions of language refers to the formal use of language. It includes parts of speech, sentence structure, spelling, capitalization, and punctuation marks. All are important to identify and know how to use because they affect the clarity of the author's message. Because they allow a writer's message to be clear, their correct use strengthens the content of a piece. Convention skills in this section include identifying and using adjectives, prepositions, and verbs for parts of speech; using varied sentence structure; and using quotation marks in conversation.

Conventions typically are presented in grammar texts and language-skills workbooks. They often are taught as rote exercises in isolation. Students practice underlining certain parts of a sentence, filling in a blank on a worksheet, or adding punctuation marks in given sentences. Demonstrating how authors use these skills to polish their pieces is a more interesting and authentic way to teach these skills.

Mastery of conventions, as all other writing skills, is developmental. By the end of kindergarten, students should be able to begin a sentence with a capital letter and end it with a period. In first-grade, students should be able to write statement and question sentences. They should use correct grammar skills, capitalization for names and the beginning of sentences, and punctuation marks such as periods and question marks. First-grade students may be introduced to quotation marks for conversation, but do not expect them to master using this type of punctuation in writing. Third-grade students learn the parts of speech and are ready to apply them with more mature vocabulary. Fourth-grade students are developmentally ready to master the use of quotation marks in dialogue. They have learned basic sentence structures and are ready to learn how to vary their sentences.

Many Luscious Lollipops models several types of adjectives. You, of course, may choose which types of adjectives are appropriate for your students' needs. Because adjectives are a part of speech we have included them in the Convention section. You may also choose to use this lesson as a prerequisite to the Elaboration section of lessons.

Use the literature books in these lessons as models to demonstrate proficient use of the skills. *Bigmama's* relates the author's boyhood memory of visiting his grandmother. This book uses prepositions in a clear, careful manner to describe the specific locations of items found at Bigmama's.

The entire story of *Anna's Rain* is a conversation. It provides a wonderful model for how to use conversation in narrative writing.

Teachers will find a lesson about present tense and active verbs in the book *Scrabble Creek*.

The varied sentence-structure lesson based on the book *Windsongs and Rainbows* allows students to see that sentences may begin with nouns or verbs and that all sentences need not be statements.

All of these books allow students to see the value of learning parts of speech, varying their sentences, and using conversation in writing.

Two other books which may be used to model convention skills are the following:

Dear Mr. Blueberry by Simon James
Up, Up and Away by Ruth Heller

Many Luscious Lollipops

by Ruth Heller

Primary Lesson

Materials:

Many Luscious Lollipops, package of jellybeans, large chart paper divided vertically into three sections, large blank sheet of chart paper, markers, pencils, writing folders or notebooks, paper

Mini-lesson:

adjectives

NOTE:

The text at the end of the book may be too complicated for younger students, but the illustrations will help reinforce the mini-lesson.

Mini-lesson

A. Build background.

Divide a large piece of chart paper into three vertical sections. Place the chart paper so that all students can see it clearly.

Write *Jellybean* at the top of the chart. Write *Looks* at the top of the first section, *Feels* at the top of the second section, and *Tastes* at the top of the third section.

Give each child a jellybean. Instruct them to look at the jellybeans closely. Ask the class for words that describe how their jellybeans look. Write their words under the *Looks* section.

Next, have students concentrate on how their jellybeans feel. Ask for words that would describe how a jellybean feels and record them under the *Feels* section. Finally, have students taste their jellybeans. Ask for words that describe how jellybeans taste. Record them under the *Tastes* section.

Reread the entire chart. Ask what the list of words would describe. Explain that the list of words just generated is a list of adjectives. Define adjectives as words that describe a number, color, size, feeling, or sound.

Ask why an author would want to use adjectives in a piece of writing. Explain these words are used because they describe something about the person, place, thing, or action in a piece of writing.

B. Introduce the book and the author.

Explain that *Many Luscious Lollipops* is an entire book about adjectives. Instruct them to listen as the book is read aloud for adjectives that they hear.

C. Read the book aloud.

Stop occasionally to review the adjectives on a page.

D. Model the skill.

Return to the jellybean chart from Building Background. Ask how many students like jellybeans. The teacher should think aloud for the class, saying, *I'm going to write an expository piece about why I like jellybeans.* On a large sheet of chart paper write the lead sentence, *I really like jellybeans.*

Ask, *What do I need to say in my piece about jellybeans?* Lead students to recognize the piece needs to explain what the teacher likes about jellybeans.

Look back to the *Looks, Feels, Tastes* chart. Think aloud saying, *I like the way jellybeans look. I will look at this chart and find some words that would describe the way a jellybean looks.*

Find two or three adjectives from the chart and use them in composing the jellybean piece. For example, under the lead, write, *I like they way they look. They can be red, green, orange, or yellow. Jellybeans are small and oval-shaped. They look like an egg.*

Divide the class into groups of three or four. Give them half-sheets of chart paper. Have each group choose a section from the jellybean chart. Have one student from each group write the group's topic choice at the top of the paper.

Direct them to write three or four sentences using adjectives that describe how a jellybean looks, feels, or tastes, depending on the section they chose. Each student in the group should write at least one sentence on the chart.

After five to ten minutes, ask groups to share their sentences. Ask the rest of the class to listen for adjectives.

Quiet Writing/Conferencing

As students begin individual, quiet writing, encourage them to include adjectives that tell more about the attributes of the person, place, thing, or action in their pieces. If they want to continue the jellybean pieces from the group activity, have them select a new sense to write about. For example, if their group wrote about how a jellybean looks, have each student try writing individually about how a jellybean feels.

If students choose to begin new pieces of writing, remind them to use adjectives in their descriptions. Caution the developing writers to be careful to use adjectives which give information that is not already apparent in the noun it modifies. For example, in the sentence, *I walked in the green grass*, the adjective *green* is not necessary because the reader already knows that grass is almost always green. A better sentence would be *I walked in the tall, wavy grass.*

This skill requires constant modeling by the teacher, along with listening to children's literature with effective use of adjectives.

Sharing

Ask at least one student who has continued the jellybean piece from the group activity to share their writing. Have the class listen for adjectives and point them out on the class chart made previously. Pick out adjectives that are especially vivid, and tell students why these words make a difference in the meaning or the author's message.

Throughout the day, have students listen for adjectives used in all genres and point out examples that are specific and appropriate.

Many Luscious Lollipops

by Ruth Heller

Intermediate Lesson

Materials:

Many Luscious Lollipops, chart paper, markers, students' notebooks and writing folders

Mini-lesson:

adjectives

Mini-lesson

Please note that there are several kinds of adjectives presented in this book. You may wish to use this book for separate lessons on the different kinds of adjectives.

A. Build background.

Review with students the importance of using details in writing to paint pictures in the mind of the reader.

Explain that many of the describing words writers use belong to a special group of words known as *adjectives*.

Adjectives are words that describe nouns—people, places, and things.

B. Introduce the title and author of the book.

Use the title as an example of adjectives describing a noun. Discuss the difference between *Lollipops* and *Many Luscious Lollipops.* The words *many* and *luscious* are examples of adjectives.

C. Tell students that as you read this book aloud, they should jot down the adjectives they hear.

D. Read book aloud.

E. Discuss the following.

Ask students to look over their lists of adjectives and suggest a category or group that several words belong to. Again, you may wish to concentrate on a particular group of adjectives, according to the needs of the class.

Record the categories on chart paper. See the sample chart which follows the Sharing section of this lesson.

Ask the students for examples in their jot lists that belong to each category. Record their responses.

Ask students for other examples that would belong to each category. Record their responses.

Choose an object in the room, and ask students to describe it by number, color, size, and or style. Share a few responses. See sample descriptions of classroom objects.

Record these on the chart and discuss where to insert a comma when using two or more adjectives together.

Quiet Writing/Conferencing

Tell students that writers need to use adjectives effectively in all types of writing. Today, they are going to practice using adjectives in an expository writing piece. Ask students to think about a special game, toy, or possession they own. Tell them to make jot lists of adjectives that describe the parts of their special possessions. Then, they should use the adjectives in complete sentences to describe their possessions. Encourage them to use a variety of adjectives in their descriptions. Caution students about the use of redundant adjectives, such as *green grass* or *sharp points*. Remind them to include the comma in the proper place.

Have students revisit pieces of writing from their folders for another activity which encourages attention to adjectives. Ask them to choose narrative or expository pieces and look for the adjectives. They may use a highlighter to mark the adjectives. This helps students see where they may need to insert adjectives in their writing to create a more meaningful message for the reader.

Sharing

As students share their pieces, have the class make note of effective adjectives. After a student shares a piece, invite the class to ask questions and offer comments about the writing.

Chart
Intermediate Lesson
for
Many Luscious Lollipops

(Use parts that are appropriate for the type of lesson you are conducting on adjectives.)

Categories of Adjectives

Number	Color	Size	Style
twelve	blue	large	gorgeous
some	colorful	universal	mysterious
few	gray		star-spangled
many	red		asteroidal
			mesmerizing
			glittering
			hard

Feeling	Thought/Idea	Demonstratives
weary	peaceful	this
wounded	universal	that
peaceful	rainy	these
wet	wintry	those
soggy		

Possessives	Articles	Proper
our	a	Persian
clown's	an	Irish
elephant's	the	
rider's		
her		
its		
his		

Comparatives		Superlatives	Irregular
curly	curlier	curliest	good
fair	fairer	fairest	better
tall	taller	tallest	best
more		most	
less		least	

Sample Descriptions of Classroom Objects

On the *chalk* ledge is *a black, fuzzy* eraser with *wavy, white* printing on top.

Her broken, yellow pencil lay on the desk in *splintery slivers* of wood and lead.

The powdery, white chalk dust made *the softest clouds* as it was erased from *Mrs. McElveen's* board.

Bigmama's

by Donald Crews

Primary Lesson

Materials:

Bigmama's, small figurine or stuffed animal, marker, sentence strips with pre-written sentences found in the Quiet Writing section, index cards and paper for each student, writing folder or notebook, pencils.

Mini-lesson:

prepositions

Mini-lesson

A. Build background.

Place the figurine in front of the book. Ask students to describe where the figurine is compared to the book. (It is *in front of* the book.)

Place the figurine next to the book. Ask where it is. (It is *next to* the book.)

Place the figurine behind the book. Ask where it is. (It is *behind* the book.)

Place the figurine under the book. Ask where it is. (It is *under* the book.)

Write the words *in front of, next to, behind,* and *under* on the large sheet of chart paper. Tell students that special words explain the location of things. These words are called prepositions.

Write the word *Prepositions* at the top of the chart paper.

B. Introduce the book and author.

Show the cover of the book. Explain that Bigmama is the name Donald Crews calls his grandmother. Although he is a grownup now, Donald Crews has wonderful memories of visiting his grandmother when he was a little boy. Because he wants the reader to see exactly what Bigmama's house looked like, the author uses prepositions in his writing to explain the locations of special objects.

Ask students to listen for those objects and for their locations as the book is read aloud.

C. Read the book aloud.

D. Discuss the following.

Ask students who heard any prepositions in the story to raise their hands.

Ask for a few volunteers to share the prepositions that they heard. Make note of any prepositions that also are on the chart in the Building Background section.

E. Model the skill.

Have the following sentences pre-written on sentence strips.

The big clock is _____ the fireplace.
_____ the hall is Mama and sister's room.
_____ to it is Bigmama and Bigpapa's room.

Put the sentence strips in a pocket chart, and read the three sentences aloud using the word *blank* in the empty spaces.

Reread the first two pages of the book aloud.

Ask students to listen for prepositions that would fit in the sentences in the pocket chart.

Choose one student to volunteer the preposition for the first sentence.

Speak each suggestion into the sentence. (*Over* is the preferred answer.)

Choose two other students to volunteer the prepositions for sentences two and three. Speak the prepositions into each sentence. *Across* and *next to* are the preferred answers.

Give each student three index cards. Ask them to write the word *over* on one card, *across* on another card, and *next to* on the last card. The teacher should write these words on index cards as the students write. Put tape on the back of each card.

Hold up the cards one at a time. Have the students read the cards aloud.

Ask for a volunteer to tape the teacher's correct word card on the sentence strip where it would belong, according to the first two pages of the book.

Quiet Writing/Conferencing

Have students find the classroom clock and pick out their index cards that read *over*. Ask them to write sentences on pieces of paper using the preposition that tells where the classroom clock is. Kindergarten teachers may need to model writing a sentence on the overhead or the chalkboard. Then have the students try it on their own. A student example might be *The clock is over the window.* Have several students share their sentences.

Ask students to find their index cards that read *across*. Have them write sentences using the preposition that tells *who* or *what* is across from their classroom or from where they are sitting. Again, you may need to model a sentence first. A student example might be *The stairs are across from our classroom,* or *The computer is across from me.* Have a few students share their sentences.

Follow the same procedure with *next to.* Have the students write sentences naming those who sit next to them. An example might be *Maddie sits next to me.* Have a few students share their sentences.

Review the importance of using prepositions to explain location. Remind students that prepositions help readers see what the writer is seeing. Use the final, hypothetical example of a little girl writing a piece about falling in the swimming pool. The story isn't completely clear unless she writes that her brother was standing behind her and pushed her in.

Provide students with lists of prepositions to keep in their writing folders, or make a chart list of these words to be displayed in the classroom. As students move into individual, quiet writing, ask them to think about the setting of the new stories they are about to begin. Remind them to use prepositions to describe where important items can be found in their setting.

If students are returning to work on previous stories, encourage them to check for prepositions. If their previous stories had no prepositions to describe the location of important objects, help students add them to the piece.

In expository writing, you can transfer this skill to the content area. Explaining where animals make their homes or setting up a simple experiment requires prepositions to provide clarity. Try using these examples in future writing workshops.

Sharing

As students share, pick out the prepositions used and find them on the class chart. To review this lesson, ask students to answer questions such as:

Who was next to you when you _____?
What was behind the _____?
How were you feeling when you went past the _____?
Where was the _____ located?

Bigmama's

by Donald Crews

Intermediate Lesson

Materials:

Bigmama's, chart paper, markers, scrap paper, students' notebooks and writing folders.

Mini-lesson:

prepositions

Mini-lesson

A. Build background.

Ask students to think about how things are organized in their homes. Where do they keep towels or food or games and toys? Share a few responses. Note how the students use prepositions in their language.

Ask students to think about what the outside of their home looks like. Does their apartment building have a sidewalk in front? Where are the trees or flowers, a stack of firewood, the garbage cans, or a swing set? Share a few responses.

B. Introduce book and author.

Tell students that you are going to share a book written by Donald Crews about his own boyhood memories of visiting his grandmother. He and his brothers and sisters called her Bigmama, so that is why he chose this title as the focus of the book. Share the author's family photo on the back cover.

Tell students that as you read the book, they should notice how Donald Crews used a clever way to help us *see* all the interesting places at Bigmama's house.

C. Read book aloud.

D. Discuss the following.

Ask students to recall one of the places that Donald Crews described about Bigmama's house or yard. After the student's response, find that part of the book, and reread the passage.

Ask students to notice what words Donald Crews used to describe the location of certain things in each place. Responses should include words like *in, over, across, next to, off,* etc.

Record their responses on chart paper. Then repeat with a few more examples of places mentioned in the book.

Explain to students that these kinds of location words are called prepositions. Prepositions are special detail words that help readers see a place or follow an event more clearly. Prepositions often clearly describe the location of items.

Use Chart One which follows the Sharing portion of this lesson to show some examples from the story. Read one example, then read it without the prepositions. Discuss the difference in meaning.

Share a few more examples. Help the students to conclude that prepositions almost make the reader feel that they are with Donald Crews as he explores Bigmama's house. Without the prepositions, much of the meaning is lost.

Compose more prepositions to add to the list. Post this as a class resource.

Quiet Writing/Conferencing

Tell students that Donald Crews used prepositions in a narrative piece of writing, but prepositions can be used in expository writing as well. Try using prepositions in expository writing by describing the location of something. Model a description of a location on chart paper using prepositions. See Chart Two, which follows Chart One. Then have students write descriptions of their bedrooms using prepositions to describe the location of items in their rooms.

Have students choose narrative or expository pieces from their writing folders and look for prepositions. Allow time for revisions. After they revise the pieces, tell the students to find a partner. Each person will take turns reading a piece and then listening to the partner's piece. Instruct the listening partner to make tally marks every time a preposition is used. This gives the listening person more practice for identifying prepositions.

Sharing

To illustrate how effective prepositions can be in description, give the students some blank sheets of paper. Scrap paper will do well.

Invite a student to share the piece of writing which describes their bedroom. Instruct the class to listen carefully and try to imagine what the writer's bedroom looks like. Then have the student read it slowly a second time, while the class tries to sketch the writer's bedroom according to the description. If the prepositions clearly described the location of items in the room the sketches generally should match the writer's spoken instructions. Invite the class to ask questions about the writing. Offer comments about the prepositions or any other words that were especially effective in helping to paint a clear picture.

Charts
Preposition examples from book
Intermediate Lesson
for
Bigmama's

Chart One

(Consider using all or parts of this chart. Or, you may make an overhead transparency instead. As you review the examples, you may wish to highlight the prepositions.)

Off the porch were three rooms. The tiny extra room no bigger than the bed *in* it. None of us wanted to sleep there alone. The dining room *with* the big round table and chairs. And *next to* it, the kitchen. *On* the porch was the washstand, where we washed our hands, faces - and feet. *At* the end of the porch was the well.

In the backyard was the chicken coop, where Sunday dinner's chicken spent its last days.

Behind the shed full *of* old stuff was the outhouse. Okay now, but scary *in* the dark.

We stopped *for* a drink *at* the pump.

We ran *past* the pear tree, where the turkeys roosted *at* night.

Under the tractor *in* front *of* the toolshed was a good place *to* look *for* nests *with* eggs *in* them.

Next to the toolshed was the huge, empty pot *for* making syrup *from* sugar cane juice.

Down the path, *past* the cow pen and the pig pen, *to* the pond. The flat-bottomed boat was still there.

Chart Two

Description of a Location Using Prepositions

(You may wish to compose a description such as the following, and then go back and underline or highlight the prepositions.)

Topic: teacher's work area

My desk is *near* a front corner of the classroom. *On* the right side *of* it is a small file cabinet, *with* shelves and supplies placed *on* top. *To* the right *of* the file cabinet is the computer shelf where I have many books, a computer, and a printer. The books I use *for* writing lessons are *on* a shelf *above* the printer. The books I use for reading lessons are *in* a blue crate *on* the same shelf, *to* the left *of* the writing lesson books. *Behind* my desk is the blackboard where I write the daily homework assignments. *On* the floor *to* the left *of* my desk is the waste basket. *In* front *of* my desk are two students desks which are the beginning *of* table #1.

Anna's Rain

by Fred Burstein

Primary Lesson

Materials:

Anna's Rain, a large index card with quotation marks, large chart of the four sentences used in the Quiet Writing section, colored highlighter, writing folder or notebook, paper, pencils

Mini-lesson:

quotation marks

NOTE:

Don't expect primary students to master the skill of quotation marks. Expect them to recognize quotation marks and to understand what they mean.

Mini-lesson

A. **Build background.**

Tell the class they will be asked a question. They need to answer the question in a complete sentence. For example, if the teacher asks, *What color eyes do you have?* The student should answer, *I have _____ eyes.*

Ask selected students the following questions individually.

What color are your eyes?
How old are you?
What is your favorite color?
When is your birthday?
What flavor ice cream do you like?
What grade are you in?
What is your middle name?

Explain that it was easy for them to tell who was asking and answering the questions because they could actually see the two people talking. But, when a character speaks in a book, the author has to use special symbols so the reader will know which character is speaking and who is speaking in return. These symbols are called quotation marks.

Show students the index card example of quotation marks. Explain that the quotation mark symbols go before and after the words that a character actually says. When two characters talk back and forth like they just did, it is called conversation. Quotation marks have to be used in a piece of writing that uses conversation to show who is taking turns speaking.

B. **Introduce the book and the author.**

Tell the class that *Anna's Rain* is an unusual book because the author uses only the words that Anna and her daddy say. It is written entirely in conversation.

Ask the students to look for the quotation marks on each page. Be sure to hold the book so the class can see it.

C. **Read the book aloud.**

D. **Go back through the book, and have a student point out the quotation marks on each page.**

E. **Model the skill.**

Write on a large sheet of chart paper the following sentences from the book.

"Are you getting bird food all over the porch?"
"Don't worry, Daddy. The raccoon will clean it up tonight."
"It's raining out, honey. You can't feed the birds now."
"Well, I have to."

Reread the sentences. Students can read them aloud as well. Ask who was talking in the first sentence. (Daddy.) Write, *Daddy said*, in front of the first sentence. You or a student could do this.

Read the second sentence. Ask who was talking in that sentence. (Anna.) Write, *Anna said*, in front of the second sentence.

Continue this pattern for the other two sentences.

Next, ask what symbols let the reader know exactly what the two characters, Anna and Daddy, said. The answer is quotation marks.

For each sentence, have a student mark the quotation marks with a highlighter.

Quiet Writing/Conferencing

Tell students to experiment with quotation marks. During individual, quiet writing, encourage them to choose a character in new or previous pieces and have the character speak to another character. For example: A story about not wanting to go to bed could be re-written to read, "Time to go to bed," said Mom. "No, I'm not tired," I said.

Remind them to look back at the chart of the conversation Anna and her daddy had. Tell them to use the same symbols highlighted on the chart to indicate what the character is actually saying in the piece. Remind them that quotation marks are symbols that allow a writer to put exact words in their characters' mouths and allow the reader to know whose words they are.

Once students recognize the quotation mark symbol and what it represents, they are able to experiment with quotation marks in their own writing. Although they may not be proficient in the use, their awareness will be raised for future lessons.

Sharing

Have a student who has tried quotation marks in a piece of writing share with the class. Have the student hold up the piece of writing so the audience can see the symbols. The author should identify the character and read what the character said. The audience can help determine if the quotation marks are in the correct place. If they are not, classmates can suggest to the author where to move them so they are in the appropriate place.

Note: If no student attempts quotation marks during this particular writing workshop, ask one of the sharing authors if there is a place in their stories where they could have used conversation. Then ask what symbol they would have used to identify the conversation.

Anna's Rain

by Fred Burstein

Intermediate Lesson

Materials:

Anna's Rain, chart paper, markers, students' notebooks and writing folders

Mini-lesson:

quotation marks in conversation

Mini-lesson

A. Build background.

Ask students if they have ever noticed that when we participate in activities with other people we often talk to one another at the same time. Brainstorm such examples as playing a game, practicing with a sports team, watching a TV program, preparing a meal, or working in the yard.

Now ask students to imagine what these activities would be like if we did not speak to each other. Instead, all actions would be carried on silently. Students will probably laugh and respond that these activities would be boring or would be difficult to do.

Conclude with students that conversation is an important part of many of our actions. In fact, conversation is often what causes us to think a certain way or proceed with specific actions. For example, while having dinner with your family each person may relate the happenings of their day. In response you may laugh or ask questions.

B. Introduce book and author.

Tell students that the book you are sharing is entirely written in conversation. It is from the conversation that students will know what actions are taking place.

C. Read book aloud.

D. Discuss the following.

Share the back cover of the book with students so they can see how conversation can provide the spark to inspire a piece of narrative writing.

Ask students how the book's title matches the meaning of the conversation.

Discuss with students what happens in this conversation.

Discuss with students how long a time period is spanned during the conversation. Students should conclude that the entire conversation lasted about ten minutes.

Guide students to see that short conversations can add interest and meaning to a narrative piece of writing

Go back and reread the book. As you read each page, ask students if they were able to tell who was speaking and how they were able to do so.

Tell students that a writer must use marks known as quotation marks to help the reader understand that a conversation is taking place.

Explain to students that they may have seen quotation marks used in other ways, but today they will be practicing how to use them in conversation.

Point out the rules for writing conversation by showing students where the punctuation marks and capital letters belong. Use the chart which follows the Sharing section. Note these examples include a statement, a question, and an exclamation.

Using the same examples, show students how to add the speaker to the beginning or ending of the quotation. This part is not shown in *Anna's Rain* but is used in all novels and students' reading basals. You may wish to post this chart as a classroom reference.

Conclude by reviewing the effectiveness of using conversation to describe action in a piece of writing as well as the rules for writing quotations.

Quiet Writing/Conferencing

Have students make jot lists of a few daily activities they participate in. Ask them to choose one in which there is conversation with another person during the activity. Examples may include a conversation at dinner the night before, a conversation at the breakfast table that morning, or a conversation in the car or bus on the way to school. Tell them to describe the action in the activity by using as much conversation as possible. Remind them to use the chart as a reference for rules to follow in writing quotations.

Encourage students to revisit narrative pieces of writing in their folders. Tell them to look for places where they may insert conversation. After they try this revision, ask them to share it with a partner or the class.

Sharing

Have a few students read their conversations aloud. To reinforce the correct way of writing conversation, have the writer choose one sentence from the conversation to reread aloud. As it is read a second time, have the class record the sentence and supply the quotation marks where they think they should go. You then can write the quotation on the board or chart paper, and students can check their work for accuracy. Post several of these student examples in the room as a resource.

Another activity for sharing examples of conversation involves choosing a selection from the students' reading basal. Find a selection with two speakers. Have the students work in partners to read the selection to each other as the characters from the story would speak to one another. Students must notice where the quotation marks appear so they know where their speaking part begins and ends.

Chart

Intermediate Lesson
for
Anna's Rain

<u>Example of a statement quotation:</u>

"Don't worry, Daddy. The raccoon will clean it up tonight."

<u>Example of a question quotation.</u>

"Are you getting bird food all over the porch?"

<u>Example of an exclamation quotation.</u>

"Don't tell me there are birds there already!"

<u>Adding a speaker to a quotation:</u>

Anna said, "Don't worry, Daddy. The raccoon will clean it up tonight."
OR
"Don't worry, Daddy. The raccoon will clean it up tonight", said Anna.

Daddy asked, "Are you getting bird food all over the porch?"
OR
"Are you getting bird food all over the porch?" asked Daddy.

Daddy exclaimed, "Don't tell me there are birds there already!"
OR
"Don't tell me there are birds there already!" exclaimed Daddy.

Scrabble Creek

by Patricia Wittman

Primary Lesson

Materials:

Scrabble Creek, unlined, white, construction paper, crayons, chart paper, index cards with active verbs written on them, writing folders or notebooks, pencils, paper

Mini-lesson:

using active verbs

Mini-lesson

A. Build background.

Have each student draw a quick picture of themselves doing something they enjoy. Give suggestions such as writing, swimming, jumping, kicking, etc. You also will need to make a self-illustration to use later in Quiet Writing.

Have students share their pictures. Either tell the class what they will be doing later with the pictures, or allow them to guess.

On a large sheet of paper, record the verb that specifies the action that each student explained. Make sure to record the verb with an *ing* or *s* ending. After each student has shared, reread the verbs on the chart.

Explain that they have composed a list of words called verbs. Verbs show the action in a piece of writing. Words that end in *ing* or *s* are called present tense verbs because they describe action that is happening at that very minute.

Many present tense verbs show lots of action, and we may also call them active verbs.

Explain that all the words on the class-made chart are present tense verbs because the pictures show the students actually doing something, whether it is dancing, playing, or sleeping. Those actions are happening right there in their pictures.

Have one or two volunteers highlight the *ing* for each verb on the class-made chart.

B. Introduce the book and author.

Explain the book is about a young girl who goes on a camping trip with her family to Scrabble Creek. The author uses many active verbs in her book. She does this so that her readers can feel like they are at Scrabble Creek too, watching all the activities of the camping trip. Ask the class to listen for those present tense verbs as the book is read aloud.

C. Read the book aloud.

D. Discuss the following.

Return to page three of the book and reread the sentence, *Sam and Steve start splashing.*

Ask students to identify the present tense verb. Remind them that present tense verbs often end in *ing* and show the action that is happening right at that moment.

On the same page, reread, *I sit in the sun with the water bubbling around me.* Ask students again to identify the present tense *ing* verb.

On the next page, reread, *I used to sleep in the little trailer with mom and dad, but tonight I am sleeping in the bunkhouse.* Ask students to identify the active verb.

E. **Model the skill.**

Have several students come to the front of the room one at a time.

Hand each student a word card containing a present tense verb. Have the students read it to themselves without anyone else seeing it. Provide help to non-readers.

Ask the student to act out the word on the card. The class should try to guess the action.

Have students generate sentences using that present tense verb. Choose one and write it on a large sheet of chart paper. Have a student underline the present tense verb.

Continue choosing a student to depict an action, and the class to guess it, generating a sentence using the present tense verb written on the card and underlining the present tense verb. Use as many cards as you like to model this concept.

Quiet Writing/Conferencing

Return to the original pictures that the students drew of themselves. Suggest that they write one to four sentences about themselves that describe them actually doing the action portrayed in the picture. Remind them to use a present tense verb in at least one sentence. The teacher should write a few sentences from the self-illustration drawn earlier. For example, if the teacher drew herself eating ice cream, she could model the sentences: *I am eating ice cream. It is spilling out of my spoon and into my mouth. It is melting, so I'd better eat it fast!*

If some students choose not to write pieces about their illustrations, remind them to try a present tense verb or two in any pieces they begin. Remind students that they can also revisit previous pieces and revise with present tense verbs.

For narrative practice, you can suggest students to write about a time when they actually did the activity they have chosen for their self-illustrations. To practice expository writing, ask students to explain how to do the activity portrayed in their self-illustrations. Both topics could be modeled in future writing workshops.

Sharing

Choose three students to share their pieces. You should compliment the use of any present tense verbs. Say, *I noticed that you used the active verb* _____. Begin a list of present tense verbs, and hang it on the chalkboard during writing workshop. When students hear present tense verbs in each other's writing or in children's literature books, you can add them to this list.

Consider binding the students' illustrations to make a present-tense verb dictionary. You can make this a reference during writing workshop.

Scrabble Creek
by Patricia Wittman

Intermediate Lesson

Day 1

Materials:

Scrabble Creek, Day 1 Chart, chart paper, markers, thesauri, students' notebooks and writing folders

Mini-lesson:

present tense and active verbs, completed in two days

Mini-lesson

A. Build background.

Ask students to think about something they enjoy doing. Tell them to close their eyes and spend the next few minutes picturing themselves enjoying their special activity. You should do the same.

Ask students to open their eyes and be ready to share the name of their enjoyable activity. Share several responses.

Ask students to think about some of the actions they do when participating in their particular activity. For example, a student may enjoy going to the beach. Some activities they may do are walking or running in the sand, slipping and sliding on the wet sand, swimming, floating and diving in the water, or riding the waves. Have several students share. Begin a list of verbs on a piece of chart paper.

B. Introduce book, *Scrabble Creek* by Patricia Wittman.

Tell students that this story, told by a young girl, is about her family's camping trip. She enjoys almost everything they do, but there is one thing she is afraid of at Scrabble Creek. Direct students to notice all the things she and her family enjoy doing on their camping trip. Ask them to record lists of the verbs used in the story.

C. Read book aloud.

D. Discuss the following.

Ask students what was so special about Scrabble Creek. Have them remember aloud the activities the girl and her family enjoyed doing, as well as the one thing the girl didn't enjoy.

Invite three to four students to share the lists of verbs recorded while listening to the story.

Ask students to circle all the verbs they wrote down that end with *ed*, or otherwise show past tense.

Take a survey to see how many past tense verbs were found. (There will be very few.)

Ask students to highlight all the present tense verbs. These may end in *s*, *ing*, or have no ending.

Take another survey to see how many present tense verbs were found.

Explain to the students that Patricia Wittman had a reason for using so many present tense verbs. Many present tense verbs show action more effectively than their past tense forms.

Use the Day 1 chart provided after the Sharing section of the lesson. Tell students to close their eyes and listen as you read one or more descriptions from the story. When they open their eyes, invite them to share what they could see, hear, or feel.

Now identify the verbs used by the author. Point out that they are all in the present tense.

Show students that past tense verbs often end in *ed*, but present-tense verbs either have no ending or an *s* or *ing* ending. (Make sure to include some non-examples such as *made, read, drove, rode,* etc. so students realize that some past-tense verbs do not end in *ed*.)

Now tell students to close their eyes again. This time read the same description, but change the verbs to past tense.

When students open their eyes, ask them to describe the difference in what they could see, hear, or feel this time compared to the original text.

Explain to students that by using many present tense verbs, Patricia Wittman made the reader feel as though they were at Scrabble Creek watching all the activities as they happened. Explain that this is a writer's technique known as using active verbs. Active verbs show action and are in the present tense.

Note: You should include present tense forms of the verb *be* (is, am, are) as non-examples of active verbs. For example, *I am curious about the monkeys,* makes use of a present tense verb but it is not an active verb.

Quiet Writing/Conferencing

You may use one or both of these quiet writing activities to practice using active verbs. The first one is expository; the second is narrative. Both topics require several days to complete. Encourage students to use the thesaurus for help with choosing active verbs.

Tell students to think about things they enjoy doing. During planning, they will need to choose their topics and identify two or three reasons why they enjoy them. If time permits, they may begin elaborating on each reason. Encourage students to use present tense, active verbs when describing the reasons.

Tell students to think about a time when they were able to do something enjoyable, such as playing certain games or going camping. Encourage students to use active verbs when retelling the times they enjoyed certain activities.

Encourage students to apply this skill in older pieces across all writing genres. This is a valuable revision skill, as it helps to build vocabulary for future pieces.

Sharing

As students share their pieces, have the class make notes of present tense, active verbs. When students share older pieces that have been revised with present tense, active verbs, ask them to read the original version first and then the revised version so the class can benefit from the improved word choice. After a student shares a piece, invite the class to ask questions and offer comments.

Day 1 Chart

Intermediate Lesson
for
Scrabble Creek

(Use parts or all of these examples on chart paper or an overhead transparency.)

Sam and Steve <u>start splashing.</u> Mom and Alice <u>skip</u> their first rocks... Dad <u>lets</u> Baby Lannie's toes <u>touch</u> the water. I <u>wade</u> out to my favorite rock. The cold water <u>tickles</u> my feet. I <u>sit</u> in the sun with the water <u>bubbling</u> around me. I <u>am</u> Princess Mossy Rock...

Sam and Steve <u>splashed</u>. Mom and Alice <u>skipped</u> their first rocks...Baby Lannie's toes <u>touched</u> the water. I <u>waded</u> out to my favorite rock. The cold water <u>tickled</u> my feet. I <u>sat</u> in the sun. The water <u>bubbled</u> around me. I <u>was</u> Princess Mossy Rock...

"<u>Beat</u> you down to the swimming hole!" Steve <u>shouts</u>. Alice and Sam and I <u>run</u> after him. Spooosh! Dad <u>pretends</u> he <u>is</u> a whale.

"<u>Beat</u> you down to the swimming hole!" Steve <u>shouted</u>. Alice and Sam and I <u>ran</u> after him. Spooosh! Dad <u>pretended</u> he <u>was</u> a whale.

Swooosh! I <u>swim</u> underwater like an otter and <u>look</u> at everyone's toes.

Swooosh! I <u>swam</u> underwater like an otter and <u>looked</u> at everyone's toes.

We <u>build</u> a campfire and <u>roast</u> marshmallows. Frogs <u>begin</u> to <u>croak</u>. Ka-work, ka-work, ka-work. I <u>don't listen.</u> Shadows black as giant crows <u>grow</u> in the trees. I <u>don't look</u>.

We <u>built</u> a campfire and <u>roasted</u> marshmallows. Frogs <u>croaked.</u> Ka-work, ka-work,

ka-work. I <u>didn't listen</u>. Shadows black as giant crows <u>grew</u> in the trees. I <u>didn't</u> <u>look.</u>

My flashlight only <u>makes</u> a tiny dot in the dark. The trailer <u>looks</u> small and cozy, but I <u>don't sleep</u> there any more. Us big kids <u>walk</u> up together. I <u>hold</u> my breath. I <u>don't think</u> about slugs or mice or foxes or bears. Snnnap! <u>goes</u> a branch in the woods.

My flashlight only <u>made</u> a tiny dot in the dark. The trailer <u>looked</u> small and cozy, but I <u>didn't</u> <u>sleep</u> there anymore. Us big kids <u>walked</u> up together. I <u>held</u> my breath. I <u>didn't think</u> about slugs or mice or foxes or bears. Snnnap! <u>went</u> a branch in the woods.

I <u>run</u> up the bunkhouse steps and <u>wiggle</u> to the very bottom of my sleeping bag. I <u>don't like</u> the noises. I <u>don't like</u> the blackness. I <u>like</u> everything at Scrabble Creek, except...the night.

I <u>ran</u> up the bunkhouse steps and <u>wiggled</u> to the very bottom of my sleeping bag. I <u>didn't like</u> the noises. I <u>didn't like</u> the blackness. I <u>liked</u> everything at Scrabble Creek, except... the night.

Scrabble Creek
by Patricia Wittman

Intermediate Lesson

Day 2

Materials:

Scrabble Creek, Day 1 Chart, students' note-books and writing folders, chart paper, markers; arrange visit to another class or part of the school

Mini-lesson:

active, present tense verbs

Mini-lesson

A. **Review the writers' term, *active verbs*, from Day 1. Using the Day 1 Chart, review the comparison of present tense and past tense verbs.**

Discuss the difference in meaning for the reader when an author uses active verbs.

B. **Tell students that they are going out to observe another part of the school.**

Instruct students to use their senses to observe all the actions going on around them. They are to jot down the actions and details supporting those actions. For example, if reading is one of the actions observed students should describe how the reading occurred. (Two girls are reading quietly together.) Remind them to use quiet observation skills.

C. **Visit two or three school sites. Spend about five minutes observing and recording at each site.**

D. **After returning to the classroom, discuss the following.**

Ask students to share some of the actions they observed in each of the school sites. Record these on chart paper.

Review each action word and discuss whether it is past tense or present tense and active. If it isn't active, write the active form of the word next to the entry.

Tell students to choose one of the school sites and write a present tense, active verb description about it. Encourage them to support the actions with details they have recorded.

Quiet Writing/Conferencing

Students will write detailed descriptions of a school site using present tense, active verbs. If time permits, they may return to the pieces begun on Day 1, or to older pieces to revise for active verbs.

Sharing

After each student shares a piece of writing, invite the class to ask questions and offer comments specifically about the action words used.

Windsongs and Rainbows

by Burton Albert

Primary Lesson

Materials:

Windsongs and Rainbows, transparency of charts, overhead, transparency marker, word cards, pocket chart, scrap paper for every student, writing folders or notebooks, pencils

Mini-lesson:

varied sentence structure, imperative form

Mini-lesson

A. Build background.

Ask for volunteers to name the five senses. Review with students that the five senses allow people to interpret the world around them. Explain that authors often use words that involve the senses to allow their readers to interpret or understand their writing better. Words that use sight, sound, taste, touch, or smell help the reader to get a better picture in their mind of the setting, the character, or the activity. Authors use these words in complete thoughts, called sentences.

B. Introduce the book and the author.

Explain that the book is about a thunderstorm. The author uses many kinds of words to explain how the thunderstorm looks, sounds, and feels. Ask the class to listen for those words as the book is read.

C. Read the book aloud.

Read the first page. Ask which words describe the sounds that come from the objects the wind is blowing.

Read the second page. Ask which words describe how the wind feels as it touches different things.

Read the third page. Ask which words explain how the wind looks when it is blowing.

Finish reading the book without stopping.

D. Take a second look.

Put Chart One found after the Sharing section on a transparency. Read the chart with the students. Ask volunteers who come up to the overhead to underline the words they recognized previously from the activity in Section C (objects being blown around).

Make note of how the words are placed in the sentence. For example, in the sentence, *Hear the wind spin the pinwheels and flap the flag* the words, *spin* and *flap* are action words to tell what the pinwheels and the flag are doing. The action comes first, then the object causing the action comes next in the sentence.

Tell students the author could have written, *I* (or *You*) *hear the wind make the pinwheels spin and the flag flap.* It would mean the same thing, but Burton Albert chose to mix his words up and change the order by beginning his sentence with an action word. Of course, you as the teacher know that by varying the sentence structure, the author has used the *imperative* form, which requests a listener to do something.

Put Chart Two found after the Sharing section on a transparency. Follow the same procedure as with Chart One, looking for words that show the action of the rain.

Remind students again that the author has used a varied sentence structure. The meaning of the sentence did not change, only the word order.

E. **Model the skill.**

On word cards write the following words: *you, feel, the, sun*

Put the words in a pocket chart in an order to read, *you feel the sun*. Read the sentence. Remove the word *you* and have the students read the new sentence. Have students identify the action word.

Ask if the two sentences mean the same thing. (They do, but the first sentence begins with a subject while the second sentence begins with an action word.)

Put these words in the pocket chart: *Make, the, steps, dry*.

Put the words in order to read, *Make the steps dry*. Read the sentence. Ask a volunteer to move the word *dry* to the front of the sentence and remove the word *make*. Now read, *Dry the steps*. Have students identify the action word.

Ask if the sentence means the same thing. Ask what is different about the two sentences. The sentence now begins with an action word.

Dictate the following sentence to the class. Have them write it on a sheet of paper. *The ball is hit*.

Ask them to move the word *hit* to the front of the sentence and remove, *is*. If your students need the visual cue, put these words on cards, and place them in the pocket chart as before. If not, remove the cards and allow them to try writing the new sentence without them.

Encourage students to help each other rewrite the sentence putting the word *hit* first.

Read the new sentence together. *Hit the ball*.

Discuss the meanings of the two sentences. Ask if they have the same meaning. Determine which sentence begins with a action word.

Give one final example, *The trees will get wet*. Have students try, if they are ready, to independently rewrite the sentence using a different word order. If they are not, repeat the activity using the cards in the pocket chart. Remind them that they can take out any words they don't need. (The correct written response would be, *Wet the trees.*) Make note that the action is followed by the object of the sentence.

Quiet Writing/Conferencing

As students move into independent, quiet writing encourage them to compose one new sentence. Allow students to cut their sentences apart to work with word order. Have them move the words around to make their sentence sound different but mean the same thing. They could also try this activity with a sentence from a previous writing workshop. Make suggestions during conferencing about which sentences would work best for changing word order. Make note of students who have composed examples of varied sentence structures.

Another practice activity is to have students record all the actions involved in a baseball game. Write sentences about baseball that have an action word beginning the sentence. For example, *Glove the ball.* instead of *Catch the ball in the glove.* This could be another mini-lesson on varied sentence structure for a future writing workshop.

Finally, for emergent writers who are struggling with this skill, you can model how to turn a statement into a question. For example, *The trees will get wet*, can become *Will the trees get wet?*

Sharing

Choose three or four students to share their pieces of writing. Pick out words in the author's piece that could be moved to change the word order without changing the meaning.

Encourage students who have composed examples of varied sentence structure to share their writing. Consider an example of Mark who began a story about how to play baseball with, *Hit the ball. Run the bases. Slide into home. That is how you play baseball.* Having Mark share his sentences provides the opportunity for the class to hear how effective varied sentence structure can be.

Charts

Primary Lesson
for
Windsongs and Rainbows

Chart One

Hear the wind
spin the pinwheels
and flap the flag.
Rattle the shutters
and slam the door.
Rustle the leaves,
tinkle the chimes,
and gently creak the rocking chairs.

Chart Two

Feel the rain
tingle your toes
and soften the grass.
Muddy the trail
and wash your galoshes.
Dampen the bars,
Smoothen the slide,
and tickle the cup of your upraised hand.

Windsongs and Rainbows

by Burton Albert

Intermediate Lesson

Day 1

Materials:

Windsongs and Rainbows, Charts One and Two, markers, students' notebooks and writing folders

Mini-lesson:

varied sentence structure of a statement sentence; imperative form

Mini-lesson

A. Build background.

Discuss with students some of their favorite places to be, such as a porch, backyard, tree fort, beach, or park.

Ask students to think of some of the things that happen in their special place, things they see or do, etc. Share a few responses.

Tell students we often describe such experiences with statement sentences which reflect what place we visited, when we visited this place, and where the place is located.

You may need to review the definition of a statement as a sentence comprised of a subject followed by a complete predicate.

B. Introduce book and author.

Tell students you will share a book that celebrates many of the little things that happen in everyday places. Ask students to especially notice the types of sentences used to describe what happens in the different settings.

C. Read book aloud.

D. Discuss the following.

Ask students how the title of the book matches its contents. Go back to the first page of text and reread it. Ask students what the setting is in this part of the book. Then discuss the action words the author uses. Repeat the above with two or three other pages of text.

Show Chart One which follows the Sharing section. Read through each author's example, and highlight the verbs. Ask students to identify where most of the verbs appear in each sentence (the beginning and middle). Choose one example and rewrite it in the traditional word order of a statement sentence which is subject followed by predicate.

Reread the examples and ask students to listen again to the word order used by the author and the word order traditionally used, subject followed by predicate. Lead students to conclude that writing the predicate before the subject may change the sentence to an *imperative,* in which the author requests the listener to do something.

Invite students to share their opinions on using a different word order in sentences. Tell students that they can *play around* with the order of subject and predicate in their sentences and pieces which may result in a more interesting sentence structure. This is one type of varied sentence structure.

Varied sentence structure includes writing different types of sentences as well as varying the word order within sentences.

Tell students that varied sentence structure is a writing skill that may be used in narrative and expository writing to create more interesting sentences.

You may wish to model writing a simple piece with a varied statement structure. Choose a topic that everyone could relate to such as getting ready for school. See Chart Two for an example.

Quiet Writing

Tell students to think again of a special place they like to be. Have them make jot lists of things they do or see in that place. Then tell them to try to expand the lists into sentences with varied sentence structure.

Encourage students to try placing the predicate before the subject of a few sentences.

For those students who may struggle with this skill, try approaching varied sentence structures in a different way. Simply show them examples of sentences from another piece of literature, such as their reading book, which include statements, questions, exclamations, and commands. Then help them develop their own examples of these four types of sentences. Guide them to see that by writing different kinds of sentences as shown by the different punctuation marks, they are varying the sentence structure, of the entire piece.

To develop this skill further, have students revisit pieces in their writing folders. They may choose drafts or finished pieces. Ask students to study the sentence structure they used. Ask them to try changing the word order or type of sentence to create varied sentences.

Sharing

As students share their pieces, have the class make notes of varied sentence structures. You may wish to have the students share both versions of their sentences—the traditional word order and the varied word order or examples of statement sentences which were revised to include other kinds of sentences. Discuss which type of sentence structure makes the pieces more interesting and meaningful.

For another type of sharing activity, tell the class to make four headings on a piece of paper: statements, questions, exclamations, and commands. Invite students to share narrative or expository pieces. As a student shares a piece of writing, tell the class to make tally marks in the correct heading for the types of sentences they hear. Most sentences will be statements. Encourage students to revise their pieces to include questions, exclamations and commands, if appropriate to the topics.

Chart One

Intermediate Lesson
for
Windsongs & Rainbows

(Use all or some of these examples on chart paper or an overhead transparency.)

Author's examples	Traditional word order
Hear the wind	You hear the wind.
spin the pinwheels	The pinwheels spin.
and flap the flag.	The flag flaps.
Rattle the shutters	The shutters rattle.
and slam the door.	The door slams.
Rustle the leaves,	The leaves rustle.
tinkle the chimes,	The chimes tinkle,
and gently creak the rocking chairs.	and the rocking chairs gently creak.
Feel the rain	You feel the rain.
tingle your toes	Your toes tingle,
and soften the grass.	and the grass softens.
Muddy the trail	The trail gets muddy,
and wash your galoshes.	and your galoshes are washed.
Dampen the bars,	The bars dampen,
smoothen the slide,	the slide is smoothed,
and tickle the cup of your upraised hand	and the cup of your upraised hand is tickled.
Sense the calm	You sense the calm.
caress the beach	The beach is caressed.
and tease the breeze.	The breeze is teased.
Await the wave	You await the wave,
and echo the horn.	and the horn echoes.
Greet the gulls,	You greet the gulls,
scurry the pipers,	the pipers scurry,
and muffle the dip of the dinghy's oar.	and the dip of the dinghy's oar is muffled.
Feel the sun	You feel the sun.
heat the pebbles	The pebbles are heated.
and dry the steps.	The steps are dry.
Toast your toes	Your toes are toasted,
and parch the tar.	and the tar is parched.
Heat the hammock,	The hammock is heated,
warm the shadows,	the shadows are warmed,
and sprint its glints across your eyes.	and its glints sprint across your eyes.

Chart Two

Intermediate Lesson
for
Windsongs and Rainbows

Teacher example of varied sentence structure:

Sound the alarm, and

grope the snooze.

Ring the alarm, but

hit the snooze.

Shrill the alarm, and

whack the snooze!

Crawl out of bed, drop

feet to the floor.

Shuffle to the kitchen, and

pour water in the pot.

Dribble orange juice in a glass,

and measure out vitamins.

Scoop cups of dog and cat food, and

sip my coffee.

Seed the bird feeders, nibble my granola bar.

Sprinkle the shower, and

Shampoo my hair.

Swallow my coffee,

brush my teeth, and

dress for school.

Find my books and keys,

Say "Bye!" to pups, and

Out the door I go.

Windsongs & Rainbows

by Burton Albert

Intermediate Lesson

Day 2

Materials:

Windsongs & Rainbows, students' notebooks and writing folders, Day 1 charts

Mini-lesson:

using observations skills and details to develop varied sentence structure

Mini-lesson

A. Review Day 1 mini-lesson on varied sentence structure by sharing one or two pages from the book and one or two examples of students' work.

B. Using the book, tell students to notice how Burton Albert began each page by referring to one of the senses:

Hear the wind...	Feel the wind...	See the wind...
Hear the rain...	Feel the rain...	See the rain...
Sense the calm...	Feel the sun...	See the sun...

C. **Tell students that they are going to visit three different sites on the school campus.**

They will spend only three to five minutes at each site and will need to observe the site using the senses of hearing, seeing, touching, and smelling. Students will jot down in their notebooks as many details as possible, especially noting the actions that are taking place. When they return to the classroom they will use their notes to write descriptions of the three sites.

D. **Visit and observe three different school sites.**

Quiet Writing

When students return to the classroom, remind them to write their descriptions using the notes gathered during the observation. Encourage them to try varied sentence structures and to refer to the senses in their description. During another writing workshop have the students apply this skill to older pieces of writing from their folders.

Sharing

As each student shares a piece of writing, invite the class to listen for varied sentences and sensory descriptions.

Recommended Professional Literature

Avery, Carol. 1993, ...*And With a Light Touch*. Heinemann.

Calkins, Lucy McCormick with Shelley Harwayne. *Living Between the Lines*. Heinemann, 1991

Calkins, Lucy McCormick. *The Art of Teaching Writing*. Heinemann, 1994.

Clark, Roy Peter. *Free to Write*. Heinemann, 1987.

Freeman, Marcia. *Building a Writing Community*. Maupin House, 1995.

Freeman, Marcia. *Teaching the Youngest Writiers*. Maupin House, 1998.

Graves, Donald. *Writing: Teachers and Children at Work*. Heinemann, 1983.

Graves, Donald. *A Fresh Look at Writing*. Heinemann, 1994.

About the Authors

Susan Anderson McElveen lives in Palm Harbor, Florida with her husband, daughter, two cocker spaniels, and a cat. She received a Bachelor of Science degree in elementary education from East Stroudsburg University in Pennsylvania. Her Masters degree in reading was earned at William Paterson University, New Jersey. Twenty-three years of teaching experience include second through fifth grades. She is currently a member of the Editorial Board for *The Reading Teacher*. Susan enjoys nature, especially the beach and hiking in the mountains with her family, arts and crafts, reading and writing.

Connie Campbell Dierking lives in Palm Harbor, Florida with her husband and two daughters. The Kansas State University graduate received a Master's degree in special education and a Bachelor of Science in elementary education. In her twenty-three years of teaching she has enjoyed instructing students in kindergarten, first, second, and third grades as well as special education. Connie currently teaches first grade in Pinellas County. She enjoys reading, boating with her family, and of course, writing.

Susan and Connie have worked together for thirteen years. Both teachers serve as Writing Demonstration Teachers for Pinellas County. They implemented a cross-age writing workshop at their school, enriching reading and writing development in their first and fourth-grade classrooms. Susan and Connie conduct school-based and county-level writing workshops. They also present workshops at the Florida Reading Association annual conference and at regional IRA conferences. They are the authors of *Literature Models to Teach Expository Writing*. Their article, "Children's books as models to teach writing skills," was published by *The Reading Teacher*, in the December 2000/January 2001 volume 54, No. 4.

Bibliography of Children's Literature

Albert, Burton. *Windsongs and Rainbows*. New York: Simon & Schuster, 1993.

Brett, Jan. *Comet's Nine Lives*. New York: Putnam, 1996.

Brown, Margaret Wise. *The Important Book*. New York: Harper Collins, 1949.

Burstein, Fred. *Anna's Rain*. New York: Orchard Books, 1990.

Carle, Eric. *Little Cloud*. New York: Scholastic, Inc. 1996.

Crews, Donald. *Bigmama's*. New York: Mulberry Paperback Book, 1991.

Crimi, Carolyn. *Scrabble Creek*. New York: Simon and Schuster, 1995.

Curtis, Jamie Lee. *When I Was Little*. New York: Harper Collins, 1993.

Heller, Ruth. *Many Luscious Lollipops*. New York: Grosset & Dunlap, 1989.

Johnson, Angela. *Tell Me a Story, Mama*. New York: Orchard Books, 1989.

Pratt, Kristin Joy. *A Walk in the Rainforest*. Nevada City, CA: Dawn Publications, 1992.

Redhead, Janet Slater. *The Big Block of Chocolate*. New York: Ashton Scholastic, 1985.

Rylant, Cynthia. *When I Was Young in the Mountains*. New York: Puffin Unicorn, 1982.

Showers, Paul. *The Listening Walk*. New York: Harper Collins, 1961.

Stolz, Mary. *Say Something*. New York: Harper Collins, 1968.

Viorst, Judith. *Alexander and the Horrible, No Good, Very Bad Day*. New York: Scholastic, Inc. 1972.

Waber, Bernard. *Ira Sleeps Over*. Boston: Houghton Mifflin Co. 1972.

Wittman, Patricia. *Scrabble Creek*. New York: Maxmillian, 1993.

Wood, Audrey. *Quick as a Cricket*. Boston: Houghton Mifflin Co. 1996.

Yolen, Jane. *Owl Moon*. New York: Scholastic, Inc. 1988.

More Classroom-Proven Resources from Maupin House

Teaching the Youngest Writers: A Practical Guide
Marcia S. Freeman

This book helps you take your K-1 students from emergent to elaborative writers. You'll get practical help understanding the stages of emergent writing, how to model writing and to set up your room, how to schedule and organize the daily writing workshop, and how to model efficient peer conferences. Included are narrative and expository techniques to teach young writers and models for managing the writing process. For kindergarten and first-grade teachers.
8-1/2 x 11″ • 142 pages • $19.95

Building a Writing Community: A Practical Guide
Marcia S. Freeman

New and experienced teachers of developing writers appreciate this comprehensive and easy-to-use resource that helps you create and maintain an effective writing workshop. More than 350 "What Works" models and techniques teach young writers style and genre characteristics, composing skills, conventions, and the many aspects of the writing process itself. For primary and elementary teachers.
8-1/2 x 11″ • 276 pages • $23.95

Dynamite Writing Ideas: Empowering Students to Become Writers
Melissa Forney

Getting started with writing workshop isn't always easy. This book builds success by making it simple. Week-by-week support eases the teacher safely through the first year. Experienced writing workshop teachers love it because it's full of new ideas. The reproducibles included save you time and trouble. For teachers of grades 2-6. 8-1/2 x 11″ • 169 pages • $19.95

Listen to This: Developing an Ear for Expository
Marcia S. Freeman

A gem of a book! Here's a concise expository primer coupled with 21 well-written, short essays that illustrate various types of expository writing. Facing-page notes hone in on the piece's Target Skill and help you teach the skill after you read the piece aloud. Writing samples include newspaper and magazine articles, letters to the editor, poems, essays, and process description. A wonderful enhancement to your writing workshop. 6 x 9″ • 128 pages • $17.95